CHRIS BAVIN

GOOD FOOD

SORTED

CHRIS BAVIN
GOOD FOOD
SORTED

SAVE TIME, COOK SMART, EAT WELL

Senior editor Claire Cross
Senior designer Saffron Stocker
Project designer Hannah Moore
Editorial assistant Megan Lea
Jacket designer Saffron Stocker
Jackets co-ordinator Lucy Philpott
Managing editor Dawn Henderson
Managing art editor Marianne Markham
Producer, pre-production Heather Blagden
Producer Igrain Roberts
Art director Maxine Pedliham
Publishing director Mary-Clare Jerram

Photographer Andrew Burton
Food stylists Tamara Vos, Matthew Ford, Kate Wesson, Rob Morris
Prop stylist Rob Merrett
Illustrators Rohit Rojal, Alok Singh, Nain Singh Rawat

First published in Great Britain in 2019 by
Dorling Kindersley Limited
80 Strand, London WC2R 0RL

A WORLD OF IDEAS:
SEE ALL THERE IS TO KNOW

www.dk.com

CONTENTS

FOREWORD

Getting the opportunity to write my first cookbook has not only been very exciting but also a real privilege. I have always loved good food and cooking from an early age, though I have never been a chef or had any formal training. I am hoping that you'll find the recipes in this book easy and delicious!

As a parent I know how hard it is to constantly produce meals that the whole family will enjoy. My house is similar to many others I know, with different needs and food preferences and, despite my best efforts, some fussy eating from my two boys. I've heard similar stories time and again all over the country. In writing this book I wanted to give you a whole range of appetizing recipes that are likely to appeal to all.

Working in the food industry for over 20 years, importing and selling fresh fruit and vegetables, has also given me a fascinating insight into people's kitchens, what they are cooking, and their everyday concerns. People want to shop efficiently, waste less food, and save time in the kitchen, so I've addressed these concerns, too.

In this book you will not only find lots of really lovely recipes, but I have also tried to make sure it's a practical and useable cookbook. Every recipe has been looked at with you in mind! How have I done this? By trying to make sure, for example, that you don't buy an ingredient only to use half of it and find that the rest goes to waste. I've also included ideas for using up leftovers, and suggestions for swapping flavours to help you build variety into your weekly meals when you feel stuck for ideas. And there are lots of hints, tips, and shortcuts to help you save time in the kitchen and become a super-organized home cook. I have even tried to minimize the amount of washing up you have to do!

My aim for this book is to save you time and make cooking as stress-free as possible so you can enjoy good food every day and still have time to spend on other things.

I hope you enjoy the recipes and the book. Thank you all!

Yours fruitfully,

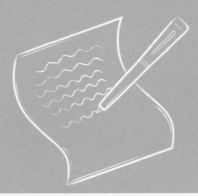

THE
ORGANIZED
HOME COOK

Smart SHOPPING

Planning your shopping helps you to cook efficiently, save time, and avoid waste. Food waste is a hot topic – every UK household throws away food, with millions of tonnes wasted each year. I've come up with a few tips to help you get organized and shop smartly, starting before you even reach the shops.

Do a weekly MENU PLANNER

Without planning, you are likely to buy ingredients that you don't use, and/or you will discover you are missing key ingredients and end up back at the shops! Plan your week's meals before you go to the shops – and try to get the whole family on board to avoid disagreements later on.

Always MAKE A LIST

List the ingredients you will need for each meal then cross off those you already have. Stick to the remaining list (provided everything is available) and you will save time and money and avoid waste.

Stock up on THE BASICS

Do one big weekly shop for basics such as oils, spices, and pasta, plus fresh ingredients for a couple of days. Then you need to shop just once more in the week for fresh goods.

Shop SOLO

Avoid shopping with others. It's all too easy to get distracted and extra bits and pieces tend to get stashed away in the trolley.

Don't shop on an EMPTY STOMACH

Try to avoid shopping when you are hungry – you are guaranteed to spend more money!

Check the DATES

"Best before", often used on dried and frozen foods, tells you when a food is past its best, but if it smells and looks fine, it is still safe to eat. An expiry date is the last day a product is thought safe to eat, so pay more attention to these.

Get to know THE LOCALS

If you have a local butcher, greengrocer, or fishmonger, use them when you can – they'll save you money and, if they do home deliveries, time. They can steer you to the best offers and most seasonal goods and introduce you to new items.

Be FLEXIBLE

Do consider swapping items on your list if this is cost-saving. If you want strawberries but raspberries are half price, use raspberries; or if you want a Baby Gem but the romaine is cheaper, can you use that instead?

IMPERFECTION is fine

Greengrocers have beautiful fruit and veg but often also have a "wonky" veg section; some supermarkets have these, too. These odd-looking items can be cheaper but are just as tasty, and easily disguised in meals.

Be wary of OFFERS

Not all offers are as good as they sound. If you need only one head of broccoli and are unlikely to use another one before it goes off, a two-for-one deal is simply a waste. It is only a deal if you need it or will definitely use it!

> **PLANNING MEALS SAVES TIME** *and avoids waste*

The organized FRIDGE

If you find yourself regularly throwing away items that have passed their best in the fridge, you may need to review where and how you're storing them and your general fridge maintenance. Randomly placed foods, the wrong fridge temperature, or less than hygienic conditions can all make your fridge less efficient. Follow these guidelines to help your fridge work at its best.

Setting the TEMPERATURE

Your fridge should be set to between 1°C and 4°C (34°F and 40°F) – that is, cold enough to keep food from going off too quickly and to stop bacteria forming, but not so cold that fridge items freeze.

Storing HOT FOOD

Don't put steaming-hot food in the fridge, but don't leave hot food sitting around for long at room temperature: bacteria can grow on meat, poultry, fish, and dairy within two hours.

CHILL YOUR Condiments

Opened jars of condiments, such as chutneys, jams, and mustards, should be kept in the fridge.

Separate RAW MEAT & FISH

Pack raw meat and fish in airtight packaging or in a clean, airtight container on the bottom shelf (see opposite) so their juices don't drip onto other foods and spread bacteria. It's especially important to separate raw and cooked foods because if bacteria does spread, this can multiply quickly when a cooked food is reheated.

ARRANGE *your fridge*

Putting items in the right place in the fridge helps to keep them fresh for longer.

- On the top shelf: cooked foods, such as ham and meats, cooked veggies, and leftovers.
- On the middle shelves: dairy, including eggs.
- On the bottom shelf: raw meat and fish.
- In the pull-out drawers: fruit and veg. Keep delicate salad leaves and herbs to the front as the colder air at the back can damage them.
- In the door: this is the warmest area, so put foods with natural preservatives, such as jams, here. Milk also keeps well here.

KEEP IT OUT

Bananas and avocados release a gas that can make some fruit and veg ripen more quickly, so keep these out of the fridge. Potatoes and onions can be kept out of the fridge in a cool, dark place. Tomatoes lose flavour when chilled so are best kept at room temperature, out of direct sunlight. And always keep basil out of the fridge as it wilts quickly in the cold.

Best FOR EGGS

Eggs should be kept at an even temperature. Some people like to keep their eggs at room temperature, but they do last for slightly longer in the fridge. Avoid storing them in egg holders in the fridge door where they can get shaken and damaged when the door shuts.

leave some SPACE

Don't overfill the fridge. This stops the cold air circulating and items can freeze if they are touching the back of the fridge.

KEEP IT *Clean*

Clean the fridge every couple of weeks ideally, using an antibacterial spray on the shelves, walls, and fridge door.

Make friends with your FREEZER

Using your freezer for anything other than ice, ice cream, peas, and fish fingers seems to have gone out of fashion, but the freezer really is the most underrated asset in the kitchen and I'm its biggest fan. Freezing food preserves nutrients and flavours. Fresh produce that's frozen quickly can actually be fresher than produce that hasn't been eaten quickly enough and has lost nutrients. Follow these guidelines to get the most out of your freezer.

The right TEMPERATURE

Your freezer should be set to a temperature of minus 18°C (0°F), cold enough to stop bacteria growing and keep foods safe.

Avoid FREEZER BURN

When air comes into direct contact with food in the freezer it causes "freezer burn", when air damages food, changing its texture and taste when thawed. Seal foods properly, squeeze out air from freezer bags, and fill containers if you can to reduce the amount of air around the food.

FILL IT UP!

Unlike the fridge, which works best when it isn't completely packed, your freezer runs most efficiently when it is full as the mass of cold food helps the freezer to keep its temperature when the door is opened. However, don't overpack the freezer as this stops cold air circulating properly.

STOP FOOD *sticking*

Freeze foods such as home-made meatballs or raspberries on a lined baking tray first, then once frozen solid, put them into a container or airtight bag, just taking out exactly what you need for a meal or dish.

Same-day FREEZING

Freeze baked goods, such as muffins and cakes, on the day that you baked them so they're frozen at their freshest and use them within three months.

Organize YOUR FREEZER

If frozen for too long, foods do deteriorate in taste and texture. Label items with their contents and the date frozen and follow these guidelines:

- Freeze a whole fresh chicken for up to 1 year; fresh chicken pieces up to 9 months.

- Freeze bacon for up to 1 month.

- Freeze fresh meat chops for 4–6 months; steaks for 6–12 months; cooked meat for 2–3 months.

- Freeze fresh oily fish for 2–3 months; white fish for 6–8 months; cooked fish for 4–6 months.

- Freeze fresh fruit for up to 1 year; veggies up to 18 months; cooked veggies up to 2–3 months.

When the POWER FAILS

If you have a power cut, keep the freezer door shut. Food stays frozen for quite a while if the door isn't opened – for about 48 hours in a full freezer and for 24 hours in a half-full one.

Defrosting BEFORE COOKING

Thawing frozen food before cooking heats food most evenly and quickly. Always thaw meat, poultry, and fish in the fridge first to stop bacteria from growing. The safest way to thaw food is to be organized and take out what you need the night before, then defrost it in the fridge overnight.

Cooking FROM FROZEN

If you do want to cook a ragu or lasagne from frozen, this is possible but the golden rule is to make sure that the food is piping hot all the way through. I reduce the oven temperature and cook frozen food over a longer period of time to make sure it is heated through completely without being burnt to a crisp on the surface.

Store-cupboard OVERHAUL

Keeping store cupboards organized can be a challenge, but a well-managed store cupboard is a real kitchen asset. You can add flavour and texture to meals at the drop of a hat, whether adding dried herbs and spices to give a sauce a flavour boost or reaching for a tin of beans to bulk up a meal when you've run out of potatoes or there isn't quite enough chicken to go around. Here are my top tips to help you make the most of your store cupboard.

Do a spring and AUTUMN SORT OUT

To keep foods at their best keep your store cupboard clean and ideally moisture-free. Twice a year take everything out, re-organize if needed, and use up older items. For example, if you have several half-used packets of pasta, put these together to make a pasta bake or a soup. Sorting through your cupboard can be a surprising source of inspiration!

look at FOOD DATES

As with fresh foods, "use-by" means an item is no longer safe to eat, while "best before", often on dried goods, means a food is past its best but can be eaten if it smells and looks fine. Bin expired foods, assess those past their best-before dates, and use up seldom-used items or give them to a food bank.

FIRST IN, first out

When you unpack your shopping and put everything away, move the items that have been in the store cupboard for quite a while to the front of the shelves and use these up before you open new packets, jars, and bottles. This will help you to keep track of what you have and avoid waste.

CHECK
the lids

Test the lids of jars to make sure that these are sealed properly and that food hasn't spoiled. If jar lids have been loose for some time, you might need to bin the contents if mould has formed or they don't smell great.

Keep an
INVENTORY

List ingredients that get used only once in a while and how much you have of each one. Stick the list to the back of the cupboard, then when you look for something like pomegranate molasses for the first time in six months you will know that you have a bottle somewhere.

Best CONTAINERS

As far as possible, decant the contents of plastic food bags into reusable containers or glass jars; this is neater and makes it easier to see at a glance exactly what's in your cupboard.

> **A WELL-ORGANIZED STORE CUPBOARD** *is a great kitchen* ASSET, LETTING YOU ADD **FLAVOUR** *and texture instantly*

Handy
BASKETS

Organize your cupboards with shallow baskets. Group together similar ingredients in a basket, such as spices, baking goods, or beans and pulses, so you know that these are all in one place rather than sprawled randomly across the shelves.

BREAKFAST

– Overnight FRUITY OAT POTS –

You can make these up the night before, in empty jam jars or pots, then chill them in the fridge to take out for breakfast on the run when you're in a rush. Use any fruit you like but the golden rule is, half a cup – a coffee cup is ideal – of oats to three-quarters of a cup of milk or thin yogurt.

Serves 2–4, depending on appetite!

Prep time: 5 minutes

INGREDIENTS

½ cup of jumbo oats or porridge oats

¾ cup of milk (dairy or non-dairy, such as oat milk), or thin yogurt

¼ tsp ground cinnamon

1 apple, grated (no need to peel)

30g (1oz) raisins

30g (1oz) apricots or dates, chopped

1 banana, chopped

some chopped nuts – I like pecans

a few blueberries, raspberries, or chopped strawberries

drizzle of honey

1 Place the oats, milk or yogurt, cinnamon, apple, raisins, apricots or dates, and banana in a bowl. Mix everything together well then pour the mixture into jam jars, or pots. Sprinkle over the chopped nuts and berries and drizzle over some honey.

2 Cover the jars and chill them in the fridge for at least 4 hours or, better still, overnight. Enjoy straight from the jar, or tip the oats into a bowl for a more leisurely breakfast.

– FLEX THE FLAVOURS –

Anything goes for this recipe – try chopped peaches, kiwi, or any other fruit you fancy. Adding a spoonful of nut butter also works really well.

- *Warm* WINTER FRUIT SALAD -

Fruit salads can be so much more than just a bit of chopped-up fruit – they can be flavourful and lightly spiced and this warmed-up one is great for a winter breakfast. Warming fruit is also a perfect way to use up fruit past its best. Try this with yogurt or porridge or simply enjoy on its own.

Serves 4

Prep time: 10 minutes

Cooking time: 15 minutes

INGREDIENTS

2 tbsp brown sugar

2 cinnamon sticks, or
  ½ tsp ground cinnamon

1 tbsp vanilla extract or paste

500ml (16fl oz) apple juice

100g (3½oz) dried apricots

100g (3½oz) pitted prunes or dates

50g (1¾oz) raisins

2 pears, peeled, cored, and halved

2 plums, halved and stones removed

squeeze of lemon juice, if using

yogurt or porridge, to serve (optional)

1 Heat the sugar, cinnamon, vanilla, and apple juice in a saucepan. Bring the juice to a simmer then add all the dried and fresh fruit. Cook on a low heat until the fresh fruit is softening but still holding its shape – which should take around 10 minutes, depending on how ripe the pears are.

2 Either eat straight away – remembering to remove the cinnamon stick first! – or, if you have time, take out the fruit and simmer the sauce on its own until it turns into a thick syrup. Add a squeeze of lemon juice then drizzle the syrup over the fruit and enjoy, or cool the syrupy fruit and store it in the fridge for up to 3 days, warming it through when you want to serve it. If you wish, serve with a dollop of yogurt or porridge.

- FEED THE FREEZER -

Freeze the cooked fruit in portions then simply warm a portion in a pan on a medium heat for 5 minutes from frozen.

- OATY BANANA AND STRAWBERRY *Smoothie* -

Fruity smoothies are a fantastic way to start the day. The addition of oats here, together with the creamy yogurt, makes this particularly satisfying – you may find that it keeps you and the kids going through most of the morning.

Makes 2 large glasses, or 4 smaller ones

Prep time: 5 minutes

INGREDIENTS
handful of oats (about 40g/1¼oz)
good squirt of honey
1 banana
200g (7oz) strawberries,
    stalks removed
big dollop of Greek yogurt
300ml (10fl oz) semi-skimmed
    or skimmed milk

1 Place the oats, honey, banana, strawberries, yogurt, and milk in a blender. Put the lid on tightly – you don't want it flying off halfway through – then blitz until everything is smooth. If you want to adjust the consistency, add more milk to loosen it or more oats to thicken the smoothie.

2 Check the sweetness and add more honey if needed, then pour the smoothie into glasses and serve them straight away for a fruity energy boost.

- FLEX THE FLAVOURS -
Any summer berries can be used in place of strawberries here – try raspberries, blueberries, or blackberries, in a combo or on their own. You can also use frozen berries out of season.

"

SMOOTHIES

are so simple

TO MAKE BUT

ALWAYS FEEL LIKE A

TREAT

– AN EASY WAY TO

PLEASE THE KIDS

"

- KALE, SPINACH, *and* GINGER *Juice* -

I often add vegetables to smoothies and juices to balance out all the sugary fruits. This juice is a great way to get some green veg into your kids – you just have to call it "The Incredible Hulk" juice! There's plenty of sweetness, too, to keep them happy.

Makes 2 glasses

Prep time: 5–10 minutes

INGREDIENTS

handful each of kale and
    spinach leaves
2cm (¾in) piece of ginger
1 mango, peeled and cut into chunks
    (or a big handful of frozen mango)
½ cucumber, cut into chunks
½ banana
150ml (5fl oz) coconut water
    or apple juice
honey, to sweeten (optional)

1 Put all the ingredients in a food processor and blitz until smooth. You can adjust the sweetness with a little honey if needed, and the thickness with a little more coconut water or apple juice, as preferred.

2 Pour the juice into glasses, ideally with lots of ice, and serve straight away.

- FLEX THE FLAVOURS -

It's easy to experiment with different fruit and veg combos.
For a flavourful juice, blitz together 150ml (5fl oz) apple juice,
1 banana, 2 tbsp oats, 2 celery sticks (optional), 1 raw beetroot,
peeled and cut into small pieces, 2 handfuls of kale or spinach,
and 100g (3½oz) mixed berries, frozen or fresh.

- AVOCADO ON TOAST *three ways* -

Avocado on toast is the current on-trend dish and for a good reason – avocados are full of healthy fats and incredibly versatile. They're often cut in price just before they get too ripe, so this is a good time to buy one if you can use it quickly. Try the following combos for a delicious breakfast.

AVOCADO ON TOAST WITH PESTO, PINE NUTS, AND POACHED EGGS

Serves 2

Prep time: 10 minutes

Cooking time: 15 minutes

INGREDIENTS

4 eggs
salt and freshly ground black pepper
drizzle of olive oil
1 tbsp pesto, shop-bought or
   home-made Pesto (see p.65)
2 slices of good-quality bread –
   I like sourdough
1 avocado, halved and stone removed
1 tbsp pine nuts

1 Fill a pan with about 3cm (1½in) water, add a dash of vinegar, and bring to the boil. Fill a bowl with cold water, ideally with some ice added to it.

2 Crack an egg into a small dish. Lower the temperature of the water in the pan so that it is only just simmering. Tip an egg into the middle of the pan and check again that the water isn't bubbling too vigorously. Cook the egg for 3–4 minutes, until the white is set. Use a slotted spoon to take out the egg and put it in the cold water to stop it from cooking further while you carry on cooking the other eggs.

3 Once all the eggs are cooked, throw away the cooking water, heat up a pan of fresh water, this time adding a good pinch of salt, and bring it to a gentle simmer.

4 Add a little olive oil to the pesto to loosen it to a drizzling consistency. Toast the bread and scoop out the avocado flesh with a large spoon then cut it into long strips.

5 Take the pan off the heat and put all the eggs back in the water for a minute to warm them through. Place the avocado strips on top of the toast, season with salt and pepper, top with a couple of poached eggs, then spoon over some of the pesto and scatter with the pine nuts and a little extra black pepper.

SMASHED AVOCADO WITH FETA AND RED PEPPER

Serves 2

Prep time: 5 minutes

INGREDIENTS

1 avocado, halved and stone removed

1 small red onion, chopped, or about 1 tbsp chopped spring onions

30g (1oz) feta, crumbled

juice of ½ lime

salt and freshly ground black pepper

2 pieces of good-quality bread – sourdough or your own preference

1 tsp olive oil

150g jar roasted red peppers, cut into strips

Parmesan shavings

1 Scoop out the avocado flesh with a large spoon and cut it into roughly 1cm (½in) cubes then pop the flesh in a bowl. Add the red onion, feta, and lime juice and mix everything together, breaking up the avocado slightly as you do so. Season with salt and pepper.

2 Toast the bread and brush one side with the olive oil. Top the toast with the smashed avocado and the strips of red pepper and scatter over some Parmesan shavings.

AVOCADO WITH SMOKED SALMON, SEEDS, AND CRÈME FRAÎCHE

Serves 2

Prep time: 5 minutes

INGREDIENTS

2 tbsp crème fraîche

1 tbsp horseradish sauce

salt and freshly ground black pepper

1 avocado, halved and stone removed

2 pieces of good-quality bread – sourdough or your own preference

100g (3½oz) smoked salmon

1 tbsp pumpkin seeds or pine nuts

small handful of chopped dill or parsley

lemon wedges, to serve

1 Mix together the crème fraîche and horseradish sauce and season with salt and pepper.

2 Scoop out the avocado flesh with a large spoon then cut it into long strips.

3 Toast the bread then place the salmon on the toast and top this with the avocado strips and a dollop of the crème fraîche mixture. Scatter with a few pumpkin seeds or pine nuts and the herbs, and serve with the lemon wedges.

- OAT AND BLUEBERRY *Pancakes* -

A stack of fluffy American pancakes is a Sunday treat in our house.
This recipe with blueberries and bananas is the ultimate. The pancakes
are perfect for popping in the freezer ready to be toasted for a super-
quick breakfast before the school run.

Makes about 12

Prep time: 3–5 minutes

Cooking time: 10 minutes

INGREDIENTS

2 eggs

175ml (6fl oz) milk

150g (5½oz) natural yogurt, plus
    extra to serve

225g (8oz) self-raising flour

50g (1¾oz) rolled oats

2 tsp baking powder

150g (5½oz) blueberries, plus
    a few extra to serve

dash of oil

3 bananas, peeled and sliced
    about 1cm (½in) thick, plus some
    extra slices to serve

maple syrup or honey, to serve
    (optional)

1 Whisk together the eggs, milk, and yogurt. Put the flour, oats,
and baking powder in a large bowl and mix these together well
before stirring in the egg and milk mixture. Once everything is
combined, fold in the blueberries.

2 Heat the oil in a pan and drop a generous tablespoonful of the
pancake mix in for each pancake. Cook for about 2 minutes and
when bubbles start to form on top of the pancakes, place a couple
of slices of banana on top then flip the pancakes over and cook
them on the other side for another couple of minutes.

3 Cook in rounds and serve in stacks of 2 per person, with a few
more slices of banana, some blueberries, a dollop of yogurt,
and a little maple syrup or honey.

- FEED THE FREEZER -

Double the mix and fry the extra
pancakes without bananas.
Stack on a tray between baking
parchment to freeze, then put in
freezer bags and toast from frozen.

- FLEX THE FLAVOURS -

Serve with a raspberry coulis in
place of the extra fruit. Gently heat
200g (7oz) raspberries with a little
honey and vanilla extract and
dollop this over the pancakes.

- SHAKSHUKA -

This Middle Eastern breakfast dish with baked eggs is the perfect solution for those Sunday mornings when you fancy a cooked brekkie, but the last thing you want to do is cook lots of different components. To get ahead, make up the base sauce the night before then just warm it up and crack the eggs in.

Serves 4

Prep time: 10 minutes

Cooking time: 20 minutes

INGREDIENTS

3 tbsp olive oil

1 large onion, chopped

3 peppers, any colour, deseeded and finely sliced

2 garlic cloves, sliced

1 tbsp Hot and Smoky Spice Mix (see p.134)

1 tbsp tomato purée

2 x 400g cans chopped tomatoes

pinch of sugar (optional)

salt and freshly ground black pepper

4 eggs

75g (2½oz) feta, crumbled

red chilli, deseeded and chopped, to taste (optional)

handful of chopped coriander

8 tbsp thick yogurt or crème fraîche, to serve

1 Heat the oil in a large frying pan and fry the onion until soft, then add the peppers and garlic. Cook for another 2 minutes before adding the spice mix. Give everything a good stir and cook for another minute.

2 Add the tomato purée, stir once more, then tip in the chopped tomatoes and simmer gently for 10 minutes, or until the liquid has reduced a little. Taste the sauce and add a pinch of sugar if the tomatoes are a bit bitter and season with salt and pepper.

3 Make 4 holes in the sauce and crack an egg into each one. Cover with a lid (or a baking tray if you don't have a lid) and simmer for 5–8 minutes, until the egg whites are set. Season the eggs with salt and pepper, then scatter over the feta, chopped chilli if using, and the coriander. Serve with a dollop of yogurt or crème fraîche.

- FEED THE FREEZER -

Double the sauce ingredients and freeze a batch. Thaw in the fridge for 2 hours and heat through, or warm from frozen over a low heat; stir through pasta for a quick supper.

- FLEX THE FLAVOURS -

Fry a little diced chorizo or bacon with the onions for an extra flavour kick.

- BLACK PUDDING HASH BROWNS
and "healthy" FRIED EGGS -

It's well worth spending a bit of extra time at the weekend rustling up this tasty breakfast or brunch for the family. Crumbling the black pudding into the potatoes gives the hash browns an intense flavour. Or make some with and some without the black pudding and let everyone pick and choose.

Serves 4–6

Prep time: 20 minutes

Cooking time: 40 minutes

INGREDIENTS

4 large potatoes, peeled and coarsely grated

1 tsp paprika

150g (5½oz) black pudding, cut into small cubes or crumbled

3 tbsp melted butter or oil

salt and freshly ground black pepper

8 rashers of bacon or Parma ham

1 tbsp olive oil

8 very fresh eggs

1 Preheat the oven to 180°C (350°F/Gas 4). To make the hash browns, put the grated potatoes in a bowl of cold water and swish them around – the water will go cloudy – then drain them. Put the potatoes in the middle of a clean T-towel and bundle them up to squeeze out any excess water.

2 Place the dried potatoes in a clean bowl. Add the paprika, black pudding, and butter or oil, then season and mix everything together until well combined.

3 Take a 12-hole muffin tin and press some potato mix into each hole, making sure the holes are packed full, then bake in the oven for 25–30 minutes, or until the potatoes are cooked and crispy.

4 Next, grill the bacon until it is crispy, or if you're using Parma ham, put this in the oven with the hash browns for 5 minutes, until it crisps up. Keep everything warm while you cook the eggs.

5 Place a large, non-stick, lidded frying pan on a medium heat. Add the oil then wipe away any excess oil from the bottom of the pan with some kitchen paper. Crack 4 of the eggs into the pan, cover with the lid (or a baking tray if you don't have a lid), and cook until the whites are set.

6 Take the eggs out of the pan and put them on a heatproof plate in the oven to keep them warm while you cook the remaining eggs. Plate up the eggs with the hash browns and the crispy bacon and serve straight away.

- *All-day* BREAKFAST MUFFINS -

I find breakfast the hardest meal in the week when I'm in a rush to get out the door for work or do the school run. Often the easiest thing to do is just grab a piece of toast or some cereal, but if you get organized at the weekend you can bake these delicious muffins to enjoy in the week.

Makes 12

Prep time: 15 minutes

Cooking time: 25 minutes

INGREDIENTS

200g (7oz) bacon, diced (or use leftover cooked bacon)

1 tsp olive oil

350g (12oz) self-raising flour

2 tsp baking powder

3 eggs, beaten

225ml (7½fl oz) milk

2 tbsp chopped chives or spring onions

100g (3½oz) Cheddar, Gruyère, or Parmesan, grated

4 tomatoes, deseeded, cut into quarters, and diced

salt and freshly ground black pepper

1 Preheat the oven to 180°C (350°F/Gas 4). Line a 12-hole muffin tin with paper cases and set this to one side. Fry the bacon in the oil until it is crispy then set it aside to cool.

2 Put the flour and baking powder in a large bowl and mix these together. In another bowl or jug, whisk together the eggs, milk, and chives or spring onions, then stir in three-quarters of the cheese along with the bacon and tomatoes and season with a little salt and pepper.

3 Pour the egg mix into the flour and stir it in well – although take care not to over-mix it. Spoon the mixture into the paper cases then sprinkle over the remaining cheese. Bake in the oven for 25 minutes, or until a skewer comes out clean, then take the muffins out of the oven and leave them to cool in their cases. Store the muffins in an airtight container for up to 4 days.

- FEED THE FREEZER -

Once cooled, freeze the muffins in an airtight container. Then whenever you fancy a muffin, just take it out, thaw at room temperature, and enjoy.

- FLEX THE FLAVOURS -

This recipe is easy to adapt. In place of bacon, tomatoes, and cheese, try 150g (5½oz) chopped smoked salmon with 1 tbsp dill and 6 chopped spring onions.

- *Smoked* MACKEREL KEDGEREE -

This versatile classic can be made for a special breakfast treat, a weekend brunch, or even a light lunch. Whenever you choose to eat it, it's the perfect way to get the kids enjoying some oily fish. It looks impressive but is actually extremely simple to make – and very delicious.

Serves 4–6

Prep time: 10 minutes

Cooking time: 20 minutes

INGREDIENTS

30g (1oz) salted butter
1 onion, finely chopped
2 tsp Indian Spice Mix (see p.134)
   or mild curry powder
300g (10oz) basmati rice
600ml (1 pint) vegetable stock
   or water
pinch of salt
100g (3½oz) peas, frozen
250g (9oz) smoked mackerel, flaked
4 eggs
2 tbsp flat-leaf parsley, chopped
lemon wedges, to serve

1 Heat the butter in a saucepan, add the onion, and cook on a low heat for 5 minutes until soft, then add the spice mix or curry powder and cook for another minute. Tip the rice into the pan and coat it in the spicy butter, then pour in the stock or water, season with some salt, and cover with a lid. Bring to the boil then simmer gently for 8 minutes, or until all the water is absorbed.

2 Take off the lid briefly to scatter over the peas, followed by the mackerel. Put the lid back on and heat everything for another minute then turn off the heat and leave to stand for 5 minutes.

3 While the rice is cooking, prepare the eggs. Bring a pan of water to the boil then carefully drop the eggs in and simmer them gently for 7 minutes. Use a spoon to take the eggs out of the pan then run them under cold water before peeling the shells away and cutting them into quarters.

4 Divide the kedgeree between 4 plates, topping each plate with a quartered egg and a sprinkling of parsley and serving with a lemon wedge on the side.

- FLEX THE FLAVOURS -

This recipe also works really well with smoked haddock instead of mackerel, adding the haddock with the peas in step 2.

PASTA, RICE, AND NOODLES

- *Quick* SPICY SAUSAGE RAGU -

This spicier twist on the classic ragu is tasty, satisfying, and quick to prepare and cook. Try experimenting with different flavoured sausages to find your favourite flavour combinations. The ragu is perfect for cooking ahead; simply reheat thoroughly and serve with pasta for a quick dinner.

Serves 4

Prep time: 10 minutes

Cooking time: 20 minutes

INGREDIENTS

1 onion, chopped

2 tbsp olive oil

2 tsp Hot and Smoky Spice Mix (see p.134) or hot smoked paprika

2 garlic cloves, sliced

8 good-quality sausages, skins removed

200g (7oz) mushrooms, sliced

good splash of white wine (about 150ml/5fl oz)

400ml (14fl oz) Tomato Sauce (see p.64), or 400g can chopped tomatoes

200ml (7fl oz) chicken stock

salt and freshly ground black pepper

400g (14oz) spaghetti or linguine

Parmesan shavings

torn basil or parsley leaves, or chopped chives, to garnish

1 Fry the onion in a large frying pan with a tablespoon of the olive oil for about 5 minutes, or until it is soft, then add the spice mix or paprika and garlic, fry for another minute, and scrape everything onto a plate.

2 Add the sausages to the pan with the rest of the oil and cook until they are a light golden brown, breaking them up with a wooden spoon as you fry them.

3 Put the onion back in the pan along with the mushrooms and fry for a minute before adding the wine. Bring to a simmer and leave to bubble gently until the wine has reduced by half, then add the tomato sauce or tomatoes and the stock. Simmer for 10 minutes then season with salt and pepper.

4 While the sauce is simmering, cook the pasta in boiling salted water according to the packet instructions. Once cooked, drain the pasta, reserving some of the cooking water, and stir the pasta through the sauce, adding some of the pasta water to loosen it if the sauce is a bit thick. Serve with a scattering of Parmesan shavings and the herbs.

- FLEX THE FLAVOURS -

Switch the sauce base for this recipe for a different type of dish. Instead of adding the tomato sauce in step 3, stir through 100g (3½oz) crème fraîche for a creamy sausage sauce.

10 *ways to* GET AHEAD

Clever kitchen shortcuts and labour-saving strategies can help you cut right down on prep and cooking times while still getting tasty, wholesome food on the table. Try these tips to help you get ahead in the kitchen.

1 Pre-chop your veggies

Get all your vegetables chopped and ready for cooking up to a day ahead. Put the chopped veggies on a plate, cover them with a damp kitchen towel to stop them from drying out, and then pop them in the fridge, ready to take out whenever you want to start cooking.

2 Blanch in advance

Cut down on vegetable cooking times by blanching vegetables first. Put them in boiling water for a couple of minutes, dip them in cold water to chill them quickly, and drain. Then just before you are ready to eat, dunk the pre-blanched vegetables in boiling water for a minute, or quickly stir-fry them in a little oil or butter to warm them through, and serve.

3 Freeze pre-prepped ingredients

Use your freezer. Freeze blanched veg and chopped raw onions; tomato- and ragu-based sauces and creamy sauces if made with double cream; and ready-to-cook meals. All can be gently reheated from frozen. Freeze garnishes, too, such as chopped herbs, chilli, and lemon wedges.

4 Pre-cook onion

Chop and fry onion ahead. Cooked onion will keep for 3–5 days in an airtight container in the fridge. (Leaving it chopped only can be a bit pungent!).

7 Ready-to-cook pastries and batters

It's easy to get ahead with pies and batters. Make pastry dough or batters up to 2–3 days in advance, then cover them in cling film and chill in the fridge, ready to roll out or cook with when needed.

5 Recruit the experts

Ask your butcher or fishmonger to do some of those more fiddly, time-consuming jobs for you, such as scaling and gutting fish or trimming cuts of meat.

9 Two-in-one meals

Cook more than you need for a dish then tweak the leftovers the following day to use in another meal. There are loads of great ideas for using leftovers throughout the book, or simply use leftovers as jacket potatoes fillers for a simple, no-fuss meal.

6 All in the pot

Opt for one-pot meals whenever possible – simply place all the ingredients in one large dish or pan ahead of time then pop it in the oven or on the hob whenever you want to start cooking.

8 Sauces to go

On days when you have time to spare, make up batches of sauces that you use regularly to freeze (see pp.64–65). When you need a sauce to stir through pasta or to serve alongside a meat or fish dish, simply reheat the sauce gently from frozen and serve – simple!

10 Get marinating

If you know a busy day is coming up, marinate meat and veggies in advance – up to a day ahead – so you can ensure that you still put something really tasty on the table.

- CHICKEN *Biriyani* -

A biriyani is one of the simplest curries to make – and the bonus
is that there's only one pot to wash up at the end. Once you've
put everything in the pan, simply leave it to bake while you
get on with other jobs, or sit back and relax!

Serves 4–6

Prep time: 15 minutes

Cooking time: 45 minutes

INGREDIENTS

2 tbsp vegetable oil

6 large chicken thighs, skin on, bone in

1 large onion, finely sliced

2 tbsp Indian Spice Mix (see p.134) or curry powder (hot if you like it spicy, mild for tamer curries)

1 green chilli, deseeded and chopped

350g (12oz) easy-cook, long-grain rice

750ml (1¼ pints) chicken or vegetable stock

salt

250g (9oz) frozen peas

To serve

small bunch of coriander

lime wedges

mango chutney (optional)

natural yogurt

1 Preheat the oven to 180°C (350°F/Gas 4). Heat the oil in a large lidded, ovenproof pan and fry the chicken thighs, skin-side down, for 8–10 minutes, until the skin is golden and crispy. Add the onion and cook for another 5 minutes, until the onion softens and starts to take on some colour.

2 Sprinkle in the spice mix or curry powder and chilli and cook for another minute, then stir in the rice, pour over the stock, together with a good pinch of salt, and bring the stock to the boil. Take the peas out of the freezer to defrost.

3 Cover the pan and pop it in the oven to bake for 30 minutes, until all the liquid has been absorbed and the rice is tender and cooked. Stir in the peas and leave the rice to stand for a few moments before serving with a good sprinkling of coriander, the lime wedges, mango chutney, if using, and a dollop of yogurt.

- FLEX THE FLAVOURS -

Make this popular curry with whichever type of meat
you like – pork or beef both work well, or use lamb for
a more distinctive, earthy flavour.

- *Quick* NOODLE SOUP -

This is my take on "instant" noodles using lots of veg and fresh ginger to give you an energy boost. For a super-quick noodle supper, keep bags of ready-prepped veg in the freezer, as well as leftover roast chicken, ginger, chilli, and lime wedges and make a double batch of the sauce to keep in the fridge.

Serves 4

Prep time: 15 minutes

Cooking time: 10 minutes

INGREDIENTS

2 tbsp sweet chilli sauce

1 tbsp white wine vinegar, malt vinegar, or rice wine vinegar

1 tsp caster sugar

2 tbsp fish sauce

1 litre (1¾ pints) light chicken or vegetable stock

5cm (2in) piece of ginger, cut into matchsticks or grated

2 tbsp light soy sauce

salt and freshly ground black pepper

400g (14oz) ramen or rice noodles

300g (10oz) roast chicken, shredded or cut into bite-sized pieces

2 heads of bok or pak choy, or a large handful of spinach

large handful of bean sprouts (blanch any left over in boiling water, cool, and freeze for the next time)

100g (3½oz) mangetout, halved

½ small red onion, finely sliced

4 spring onions, finely sliced

1 red chilli, deseeded and finely chopped

small bunch of coriander, roughly chopped

1 lime, cut into wedges

1 Pour the sweet chilli sauce into a medium saucepan then add the vinegar and sugar and place over a medium heat, stirring everything together well.

2 Once the sugar has dissolved and the sauce started to bubble, add the fish sauce then take the pan off the heat. At this point you can store the sauce in a jar in the fridge for up to 1 week.

3 Pour the stock, ginger, soy sauce, and the chilli and fish sauce into a saucepan. Bring everything to the boil and simmer gently for 5 minutes, then season to taste and add more soy if needed.

4 Add the noodles and simmer for 2 minutes, then add the chicken, bok or pak choy, bean sprouts, and mangetout. Simmer for another 2 minutes then serve in 4 deep bowls. Scatter over the sliced red onion and spring onions and the chopped chilli and coriander and serve with a wedge of lime on the side.

- FLEX THE FLAVOURS -

It's very easy to adapt this dish – with your preferred veggies and herbs or simply using up what's in the fridge. Try adding peas instead of bean sprouts, using kale instead of bok choy, or sprinkling over parsley instead of coriander.

- BACON, MUSHROOM, and COURGETTE Spicy TOMATO Pasta Bake -

Pasta bakes can be a reminder of school or student days – with overcooked, sticky pasta served in a dried-up sauce. The secret is to cook the pasta for a few minutes less than the packet suggests and to make sure that the sauce is loose enough before baking – do this and you'll end up with a delicious dish!

Serves 4

Prep time: 20 minutes

Cooking time: 25 minutes

INGREDIENTS

250g (9oz) short pasta shapes, such as conchiglie, penne, or rigatoni

salt and freshly ground black pepper

1 onion, finely chopped

2 tbsp olive oil

1 tbsp red chilli, deseeded and chopped, or 1 tsp chilli flakes

200g (7oz) smoked bacon, diced

2 garlic cloves, sliced

200g (7oz) mushrooms, quartered

600ml (1 pint) Tomato Sauce (see p.64) or passata, or 2 x 400g cans chopped tomatoes

2 medium-sized courgettes, cut into bite-sized pieces

50g (1¾oz) pitted olives, halved lengthways

4 tomatoes, sliced

1 ball mozzarella

2 tbsp grated Parmesan

basil leaves (optional)

1 Preheat the oven to 190°C (375°F/Gas 5). Boil the pasta in salted water for 2 minutes less than instructed on the packet.

2 Fry the onion in the oil for 2 minutes then add the chilli and bacon and fry for another 5–7 minutes, until the bacon is crispy. Add the garlic and stir this in then add the mushrooms and fry until they start to soften. Finally add the tomato sauce or tomatoes and bring everything to a simmer then stir in the courgettes and olives.

3 Drain the pasta, reserving some of the cooking water, and stir the pasta into the sauce. Check the seasoning and add a little cooking water to loosen everything – you don't want the sauce to be too thick and sticky at this stage – then tip the pasta and sauce into an ovenproof dish.

4 Lay the sliced tomatoes on top of the pasta, tear over the mozzarella, and sprinkle over the Parmesan, then pop the dish in the oven for 15 minutes, until piping hot. If you have some basil leaves to hand, sprinkle these over the top to serve.

- FEED THE FREEZER -

Make double the amount of sauce and freeze it in portions then thaw it overnight in the fridge before heating it through on the hob, or heat it slowly on a low heat straight from the freezer. Serve with pasta or cooked chicken.

- Weekday **PAELLA** -

Those with Spanish roots will be shouting at the page right now as this is not the classic way to cook paella, which is traditionally cooked for much longer and with more ingredients. However, this quick-to-rustle-up mid-week alternative is perfect for when you fancy a little bit of Spain on your table.

Serves 4–6

Prep time: 10 minutes

Cooking time: 30 minutes

INGREDIENTS

1 tbsp olive oil

100g (3½oz) chorizo, sliced

1 onion or leek, chopped

1 garlic clove, chopped

½ tbsp sweet smoked paprika

1 tbsp tomato purée

pinch of saffron (optional), soaked in 1 tbsp water

200g (7oz) roasted peppers (cooked and frozen then thawed or from a jar), sliced

300g (10oz) paella rice

900ml (1½ pints) boiling chicken stock

200g (7oz) frozen shelled and de-veined raw king prawns, thawed for 2 hours

150g (5½oz) frozen peas

salt and freshly ground black pepper

2 tbsp flat-leaf parsley, chopped

lemon wedges, to serve

1 Heat the olive oil in a shallow casserole dish with a lid. Fry the chorizo and onion or leek for 5 minutes, until the onion or leek is soft and the chorizo has released its oil.

2 Add the garlic and paprika and fry for another minute before stirring in the tomato purée and saffron. Add the peppers and rice to the pan and stir everything well to coat the rice in the oil.

3 Pour in the stock and cover with the lid, then lower the heat and simmer for 20 minutes, checking occasionally that the rice is not drying out or burning. Add the prawns and peas then cover again and cook for another 5 minutes.

4 Take the dish off the heat, season well, top with the parsley, and serve with some lemon wedges.

- LOVE YOUR LEFTOVERS -

Once any leftover rice has cooled, shape it into thin patties, dust them in flour, and fry until crispy on the outside and hot in the middle. These are delicious with a poached egg for a light supper or lunch.

- Quick and easy CREAMY PASTA -

Smoked salmon is not only delicious eaten cold or on its own, but it's also fantastic to cook with as it's packed with flavour so just a small amount goes a long way. Cooked in under half an hour, this is a simple but delicious treat for busy days.

Serves 4

Prep time: 20 minutes

Cooking time: 20 minutes

INGREDIENTS
350g (12oz) pasta of your choice
salt and freshly ground black pepper
2 red onions, sliced
3 tbsp olive oil
2 garlic cloves, chopped
about 250g (9oz) salmon fillet, skinned
    and cut into 2cm (¾in) cubes, or
    leftover cooked salmon
150ml (5fl oz) double cream
100g (3½oz) smoked salmon,
    cut into strips
200g (7oz) frozen peas
2 tbsp dill, chopped
zest of 1 lemon

1 Cook the pasta in a pan of salted boiling water for a minute less than the packet instructions.

2 While the pasta is cooking, in a large frying pan fry the onions in the oil for 3–4 minutes, or until they are starting to soften, then add the garlic and the salmon fillet.

3 Cook everything for 2 minutes then stir in the double cream and heat gently for 5 minutes, taking care not to break up the salmon too much. Stir in the smoked salmon and the peas and warm everything through before adding the dill and the lemon zest and seasoning with plenty of black pepper and salt to taste.

4 Drain the pasta (keeping aside some of the cooking water) and stir the pasta through the sauce. If the sauce is too thick and sticky add some pasta water to loosen it, then serve immediately.

- FLEX THE FLAVOURS -
Crème fraîche can easily be substituted for double cream and you can also use parsley instead of dill. Stirring a tablespoon of wholegrain mustard through the pasta sauce works nicely, too.

- PRAWN and SUMMER VEGETABLE Risotto -

It takes around 20 minutes to make a risotto – plus lots of stirring!
But risottos are incredibly simple to make and you can easily adapt
them with different flavours and ingredients.

Serves 4

Prep time: 15 minutes

Cooking time: 20 minutes

INGREDIENTS

3 tbsp olive oil

1 onion, peeled and finely chopped

400g (14oz) arborio rice

150ml (5fl oz) white wine

1.2 litres (2 pints) good-quality hot
fish, shellfish, or vegetable stock

200g (7oz) shelled and de-veined raw
king prawns, fresh, or frozen and
thawed for 2 hours

1 courgette, cut into 1cm (½in) chunks

3 spring onions, fresh or frozen, sliced

200g (7oz) frozen peas

2cm (¾in) disc of Garlic and Herb Butter
(see p.116), or 30g (1oz) salted butter

80g (2¾oz) Parmesan, finely grated,
plus extra to garnish

salt and white pepper

2 tbsp chopped herbs, such as
parsley, mint, dill, and chives

zest of 1 lemon

1 Heat the olive oil in a large frying pan, add the onion, and fry
for a couple of minutes, until soft but not browned. Add the rice
and stir well, then pour in the wine and allow it to bubble and
almost evaporate.

2 Add a ladleful of stock and stir constantly until it has all been
absorbed, before adding another ladle. Repeat this process
until three-quarters of the stock has been used up then add the
prawns and cook for 2 minutes, until they turn pink, stirring all
the time and adding more stock as needed.

3 Add the courgette and cook for 4–5 minutes, then tip in the
spring onions and the peas, stirring all the time and adding
more stock until the rice is cooked but still has a bit of texture.

4 Take the pan off the heat and stir in the butter and Parmesan.
If the risotto becomes too thick add a little more stock so it has
a slightly runny consistency. Finally, check the seasoning and stir
through the herbs, then serve straight away with a little more
grated Parmesan and lemon zest.

- FEED THE FREEZER -

Cook the risotto up to the point
where you add the prawns, then
cool quickly and freeze. Thaw in the
fridge, warm in a pan, and carry on
from where you left off.

- FLEX THE FLAVOURS -

Cook piles of grated Parmesan on
a lined baking tray for 3–5 minutes
at 180°C (350°F/Gas 4) until golden,
cool slightly, then serve with the
risotto to add a nutty flavour.

- LOVE YOUR LEFTOVERS -

Use any leftover risotto to make
the Crispy Arancini Balls
on page 188.

- PAD *Thai* -

Everybody in Thailand has their own slightly different version of Pad Thai. Some make it with chicken, others with prawns, while some throw both in. Some favour sweet over salty flavours or vice versa. Use this recipe as a guide, then play around with ingredients to find your own favourite version.

Serves 4

Prep time: 10 minutes

Cooking time: 15 minutes

INGREDIENTS

250g (9oz) flat rice noodles
1 small red onion, finely sliced
1 garlic clove, chopped
3 tbsp rapeseed oil
16 shelled and de-veined raw king prawns, fresh, or frozen and thawed for 2 hours
3 tbsp tamarind paste or lime juice
2 tbsp tomato ketchup (not authentic, but easy to get hold of)
3 tbsp fish sauce
1 tbsp brown or white sugar
16 small scallops, fresh or frozen
1 red chilli, deseeded and chopped
4 spring onions, chopped
2 eggs, beaten

To serve

50g (1¾oz) salted nuts, such as peanuts, chopped
small bunch of coriander
lime wedges

1 Place the noodles in a bowl then submerge them in a kettleful of boiling water and leave to soak for 10 minutes.

2 In the meantime, fry the onion and garlic with the oil in a wok – or large frying pan – over a medium–high heat for 2 minutes, or until lightly browned.

3 Add the prawns and fry for a minute until they start to turn pink, then stir in the tamarind or lime juice, ketchup, fish sauce, and sugar. Mix everything well then stir in the scallops. If you are cooking the scallops from frozen, cook them for 2 minutes before adding the noodles. Drain the noodles and add them to the pan along with the chilli and spring onions. Cook for another minute then push everything to one side of the pan.

4 Crack the eggs into the clear part of the pan and use a spatula to break them up as they cook. Once the eggs start to scramble, stir in the noodles. Cook for another 2 minutes then serve with the nuts and coriander scattered over and big wedges of lime.

- LOVE YOUR LEFTOVERS -

Keep any leftover noodles and if you have leftover meat from your Sunday roast, simply chop it up and fry it with the noodles. If you had a pork roast, finely chop up any crackling and sprinkle it over the noodles for added crunch.

5 *super-useful* SAUCES AND STOCKS

Sauces can be transformed into a whole range of delicious dishes, while a good, flavourful home-made stock is hard to beat. Stock up the freezer with these base sauces and stocks.

1 Tomato Sauce

This delicious tomato sauce takes just half an hour to cook and can be used on pizza bases, as a pasta sauce, for chicken dishes, and more. I've given quantities here for 3 batches, each serving 4.

4 tbsp rapeseed oil • 4 sliced garlic cloves • 3 x 400g cans chopped tomatoes • handful of basil leaves • pinch of sugar (optional) • salt and freshly ground black pepper

Heat the oil in a large saucepan. Fry the garlic for 1 minute then add the tomatoes and basil. Simmer gently for 30 minutes until reduced slightly. Taste, and if bitter add a little sugar. Season to taste. Cool then divide into portions to freeze. Thaw in the fridge overnight or warm gently in a pan until piping hot through.

2 My Best Ragu

Okay, so we can all cook a spag bol, but this ragu made with a combo of beef and pork really is good and can be used in a whole range of dishes. This makes 3 batches, each serving 4.

2 tbsp olive oil • 1 onion, finely sliced • 2 carrots, grated or finely chopped • 2 celery sticks, finely chopped • 2 garlic cloves, crushed • 2 tbsp Mediterranean Herb and Spice mix (see p.135) • 1kg (2¼lb) minced beef • 500g (1lb 2oz) minced pork • 3 tbsp tomato purée • 100ml (3½fl oz) red wine • 2 x 400g cans chopped tomatoes • 500ml (16fl oz) beef stock • 100ml (3½fl oz) milk (optional)

Heat the oil on a low heat. Add the onion, carrots, and celery, and fry for 10 minutes, or until soft. Add the garlic and spice mix. Crumble in the minced beef and pork and fry until lightly browned. Add the tomato purée and cook for 2 minutes. Pour in the red wine and simmer for 5 minutes. Add the chopped tomatoes and beef stock; simmer gently for 1½ hours, adding more stock if too dry. Finally, if you wish, stir in the milk to enhance the texture, cover, and cook for 30 minutes. Season to taste. Cool then divide into portions to freeze. Thaw in the fridge overnight or warm gently in a pan until piping hot through.

Pesto

Add aromatic, nutty pesto to pasta or drizzle on chicken or veggies for flavour intensity.

½ garlic clove • 100g (3½oz) bunch of basil, thicker stalks removed • olive oil • 30g (1oz) pine nuts • 30g (1oz) Parmesan, grated • freshly ground black pepper

Place the garlic and basil in a mortar and pestle or food processor and crush or blitz to a smooth paste; add a little oil to help it along. Once it's as smooth as possible, add the pine nuts, blitz again, and add a bit more oil. Add the Parmesan, blend, then enough oil to reach the desired consistency. Season. Store in an airtight container, with a tbsp oil on top of the pesto, in the fridge for a week, or freeze in ice-cube trays and reheat gently from frozen.

Vegetable Stock

Add this vegetarian stock to soups, sauces, and risottos, and feel free to adjust the amount of vegetables to use up what's in the fridge.

1 tbsp olive oil • 3 large carrots, roughly chopped • 2 leeks • 2 garlic cloves • 4 celery sticks, roughly chopped • 2 onions, roughly chopped • small bunch of herbs, such as rosemary, parsley, and bay leaves • a few black peppercorns

Heat the oil in a large pan. Add the carrots, leeks, garlic, celery, and onions, Fry the vegetables for 10 minutes, until they take on colour. Cover with 5 litres (10 pints) hot or cold water, add the herbs and peppercorns, and bring to the boil. Reduce to a rolling simmer and simmer for 1 hour, until the water has reduced by half. Pass through a sieve to use straight away or reduce further and pour into ice-cube trays to freeze, then rehydrate with hot water or add to a sauce as needed.

Chicken Stock

The vegetable quantities here are a rough guide. Use this flavoursome stock in soups, risottos, and sauces.

2 chicken caracasses • 2 large carrots, roughly chopped • 2 garlic cloves • 4 celery sticks, chopped • 2 onions, chopped • small bunch of herbs, such as rosemary, parsley, and bay leaves • a few black peppercorns

In a large pan, place the chicken carcasses, carrots, garlic, celery, onions, herbs, peppercorns, and 5 litres (10 pints) cold water. Bring to the boil then skim off any scum on the surface. Reduce to a rolling simmer and simmer for 3 hours. If using fresh, sieve the stock at this point and use as required. If freezing, reduce it significantly then pass through a sieve and pour the concentrated stock into ice-cube trays. Pop out a cube as needed and add hot water to water it down, or simply add to a sauce.

- PRAWN, CHILLI, and ROCKET LINGUINE -

The great thing about prawns is that they are super-quick to cook but feel like a real treat. This recipe uses my Anchovy and Chilli Butter but you can use any of the other butters on pages 116–17, or just use a little butter and a bit of fresh or frozen chilli instead.

Serves 4

Prep time: 10 minutes

Cooking time: 20 minutes

INGREDIENTS
250g (9oz) linguine
salt and freshly ground black pepper
1 tbsp olive oil
2cm (¾in) disc Anchovy and Chilli
  Butter (see p.116)
1 tsp chilli, finely chopped (optional)
400g (14oz) shelled and de-veined raw
  king prawns, fresh, or frozen and
  thawed for 2 hours
300g (10oz) cherry tomatoes, halved
100ml (3½fl oz) white wine
1 large courgette, grated
2 large handfuls of rocket

1 Cook the pasta in boiling salted water. Heat the oil and butter in a frying pan then add the chilli and cook this for a minute. Add the prawns, tomatoes, and white wine and simmer until the prawns have turned pink, then season with salt and pepper.

2 Drain the pasta, keeping back a little of the cooking water. Add the pasta to the sauce and mix these together – if the sauce is too thick add a little of the reserved water.

3 Take the pan off the heat and stir in the courgette. After a minute, stir in the rocket, allowing it to wilt slightly, then check the seasoning once more and serve.

- FLEX THE FLAVOURS -

Try adding some mussels and clams along with the white wine – just cover the pan with a lid or baking tray to let them steam.

- SPINACH, PESTO, and MUSHROOM lasagne -

This deliciously creamy meat-free lasagne is perfect for filling up the freezer – either freeze as one big family meal or divide it up into portions for more flexibility. The fleshy-textured mushrooms – use white or brown as you prefer – make this a really satisfying dish.

Serves 4-6

Prep time: 45 minutes

Cooking time: 35-40 minutes

INGREDIENTS

500g tub mascarpone

190g jar pesto (the best quality you can get) or home-made Pesto (see p.65)

250g (9oz) ricotta

salt and freshly ground black pepper

2 tbsp olive oil

300g (10oz) mushrooms, thickly sliced

6 spring onions, sliced

400g bag of spinach, roughly chopped, or frozen and defrosted, excess water squeezed out

150g (5½oz) frozen peas

100g (3½oz) Parmesan, grated

whole nutmeg, freshly grated (optional)

a little milk

12 lasagne sheets

2 tbsp pine nuts (optional)

a few basil leaves, to serve

1 Preheat the oven to 180°C (350°F/Gas 4). In a bowl mix together half the mascarpone and the pesto and ricotta. Season with salt and pepper then add 200ml (7fl oz) of water and stir well.

2 In a large frying pan, heat the oil then fry the mushrooms for 3–4 minutes, until golden brown. Add the spring onions, spinach, and peas and cook until the spinach has wilted, then season everything.

3 Mix the remaining half of the mascarpone with half of the Parmesan and the nutmeg, if using. Add enough milk, about 100ml (3½fl oz), to make a mixture the consistency of a white sauce.

4 Spread a little of the pesto mixture on the base of a dish roughly 18cm x 25cm (7 x 10in) then top with a layer of lasagne sheets. Scatter over some of the mushroom and spinach mix, followed by more of the pesto mix then more lasagne sheets and repeat until everything is used up, finishing with a layer of lasagne sheets. Pour over the mascarpone and Parmesan mix and sprinkle with the remaining Parmesan and the pine nuts, if using. Bake in the oven for 35–40 minutes, until golden on top and bubbling, and scatter over some basil leaves to serve.

- FEED THE FREEZER -

Make up the lasagne and cook it for just 25 minutes, then cool and freeze it whole or in portions. Either cook it in the oven straight from frozen – 1 hour for a portion or a bit longer for a whole dish, until heated through – or thaw overnight in the fridge, and bake a portion for 30 minutes or a whole dish for 40 minutes.

- CHA HAN *Rice* -

Cha Han – Oriental fried rice – is traditionally cooked in a wok but a large frying pan will do. It's easy to adapt this recipe; just throw in any veg you like. It's also great for using up leftover rice – if you do use previously cooked rice, make sure it has been chilled and use it within 24 hours.

Serves 2

Prep time: 15 minutes

Cooking time: 15 minutes

INGREDIENTS

250g (9oz) cooked rice (freshly cooked or reheated leftover rice)

1 chicken breast, cut into strips

3 tbsp Yakitori, oyster, or hoisin sauce

2 tbsp vegetable oil

8 shelled and de-veined raw king prawns, fresh, or frozen and thawed for 2 hours

6 chestnut mushrooms, cut into quarters

handful of mangetout, thinly sliced

3 tbsp canned sweetcorn or thawed frozen corn

3 eggs

1 tbsp soy sauce

coriander, 2 spring onions, chopped, lime wedges, and chilli sauce, to serve (all optional)

1 Cook the rice according to the packet instructions (or reheat pre-cooked chilled rice thoroughly). Put the chicken in a bowl, add the sauce, and toss together so the chicken is well-coated. Leave the chicken to marinate for 10 minutes.

2 Heat a little of the oil in a saucepan and add the chicken and the prawns. Cook for 3 minutes, or until both are cooked through, then tip the chicken and prawns onto a plate.

3 Put the pan back on the heat and add a little more oil then fry the mushrooms, mangetout, and sweetcorn for 2 minutes. Beat one of the eggs and pour it into the pan, stirring it constantly so that it breaks up, then add the cooked rice.

4 Add the soy sauce and stir everything together so that all the ingredients are well combined. Pop the chicken and prawns back in the pan with the rice, cover with a lid, then lower the heat to keep everything warm.

5 Heat a frying pan on a high heat. Add the rest of the oil and fry the remaining 2 eggs until the whites are set but the yolks are still runny. Serve the Cha Han in bowls, each topped with a fried egg and your choice of topping – scatter over the coriander and spring onions and add the chilli sauce and lime wedges as desired.

- FLEX THE FLAVOURS -

If you have leftover roast pork, use this instead of the chicken. Sliced beef steak is also a good chicken substitute for this dish.

MEAT

- Herb-crusted LAMB -
WITH CREAMY BUTTERBEANS AND LEEKS

This is a great alternative to the more traditional Sunday lunch – of course, a leg of lamb doesn't have to be roasted only on a Sunday, so this is also ideal for occasions when you have lots of mouths to feed. The beans are a handy store-cupboard standby to rustle up for a quick side dish.

Serves 8

Prep time: 10 minutes

Cooking time: 1 hour 30 minutes, plus resting

INGREDIENTS

1 leg of lamb, about 2kg/4½lb, bone in
1–2 garlic bulbs
75g (2½oz) Herby Breadcrumbs
 (see p.135)
30g (1oz) Parmesan, finely grated
2 tbsp olive oil
2 tbsp Dijon or English mustard

For the beans
3 leeks, sliced
1 tbsp thyme leaves
2 tbsp olive oil
2 garlic cloves, crushed
2 x 400g cans butter beans or
 cannellini beans, drained
splash of white wine (3½ tbsp or less),
 if you have it to hand
100ml (3½fl oz) chicken or
 vegetable stock
100ml (3½fl oz) double cream, or
 3 tbsp crème fraîche
salt and freshly ground black pepper

1 Preheat the oven to 200°C (400°F/Gas 6). Place the lamb on a large roasting tray together with 1–2 whole garlic bulbs and pop it in the oven for 1 hour, reducing the temperature to 180°C (350°F/Gas 4) when you put the lamb in.

2 Mix the herby breadcrumbs, Parmesan, and oil together. Take the lamb out of the oven and brush its surface with the mustard, then carefully press the breadcrumbs onto the mustard – it doesn't matter if some crumbs fall off into the pan. Put the lamb back in the oven and cook for another 20–30 minutes.

3 While the lamb is cooking, fry the leeks and thyme in the oil until they are soft. Add the garlic and cook for another minute, then add the beans, warming these through for 2 minutes before adding the wine, if using. Simmer gently until the wine has almost evaporated then pour in the stock and the cream or crème fraîche. Simmer very gently for another 5 minutes then season with salt and pepper. Take off the heat and set to one side.

4 Once the lamb is cooked, take it out of the oven and leave it to rest for 20 minutes. Break up the roasted garlic bulbs and serve the lamb with garlic cloves and the creamy beans.

- LOVE YOUR LEFTOVERS -
Shred the lamb with its herby crust. Fry a sliced onion and pepper, add black olives and the lamb, and heat through. Put diced tomatoes and cucumber on a tortilla. Add the lamb, Tzatziki or yogurt with mint, and if you have it, crumbled feta. Wrap it up and enjoy!

- Slow-roasted LAMB SHOULDER -
WITH PEPPERS AND TOMATOES

A few years back, we had a ridiculously hot Easter Sunday so our traditional roast lamb shoulder seemed a little out of place while we sat in the garden! After a quick rummage through the veg tray I came up with this – a much lighter version of roast lamb, but very easy to make thanks to the long, slow roast.

Serves 6

Prep time: 20 minutes

Cooking time: 4 hours

INGREDIENTS

1 shoulder of lamb, about 2kg (4½lb), bone in
salt and freshly ground black pepper
3 red peppers, deseeded and sliced
2 red onions, sliced
500g (1lb 2oz) cherry tomatoes on the vine
4 garlic cloves, sliced
2 tbsp balsamic vinegar
6 sprigs of rosemary

For the potatoes
1 kg (2¼lb) new potatoes
1 tbsp olive oil
zest of 1 lemon
squeeze of lemon juice

For the crème fraîche dressing
200ml (7fl oz) crème fraîche
2 tbsp harissa paste or chilli paste
1 tbsp sweet chilli sauce
salt and freshly ground black pepper

1 Preheat the oven to 220°C (425°F/Gas 7). Place the lamb in a large roasting tray with plenty of room around it and season well with salt and pepper, then put it in the oven, turn the oven down to 160°C (325°F/Gas 3) straight away, and roast for 2 hours.

2 Take the lamb out of the oven and drain or spoon off excess fat. Add the peppers, onions, tomatoes, and garlic to the tray, season with salt and pepper, drizzle over the vinegar, and add the rosemary. Pop it back in the oven and roast for another 2 hours.

3 Boil the potatoes until tender. Once cooked, drain well then put them back in the pan and add the olive oil, lemon zest, and a squeeze of juice. Season with salt and pepper.

4 To make the dressing, simply mix together all the ingredients to achieve a smooth consistency.

5 Serve the lamb with the roasted peppers and other vegetables, the lemony new potatoes, and the spicy dressing.

- LOVE YOUR LEFTOVERS -

There are plenty of ways to use up leftover lamb here. Use it in place of the beef in the stir-fry on page 87, or substitute it for the chicken in the curry on page 102. Alternatively, toss with roast veg, couscous, and a dressing for a simple supper.

- LAMB CHOPS -
WITH AUBERGINE AND CHICKPEAS

This delicious flavour combo is simple to rustle up for a satisfying mid-week dinner and also makes an ideal dinner party dish. The aubergine and chickpea stew tastes even better made a day ahead – just chill the stew in the fridge then reheat it while you grill the lamb chops.

Serves 4

Prep time: 10 minutes

Cooking time: 25 minutes

INGREDIENTS

2 large aubergines, cut into
   1cm (½in) cubes
3 tbsp olive oil
salt and freshly ground black pepper
8 lamb chops
1 garlic clove, finely chopped
pinch of red chilli flakes
400g (14oz) cherry tomatoes, halved
3½ tbsp white wine
100ml (3½fl oz) vegetable stock
400g can chickpeas, drained

1 Fry the aubergines in a little of the oil with a pinch of salt until they are golden brown.

2 While the aubergines are cooking, rub the lamb chops with the remaining oil, season with salt and pepper, then put them under the grill. Cook the chops for 4 minutes on both sides, then set aside to rest for 5 minutes.

3 Add the garlic and chilli to the aubergines and fry for 30 seconds, then add the tomatoes and pour in the wine. Simmer for about 5 minutes, until the liquid has almost evaporated, then pour in the stock and add the chickpeas. Warm everything through, season to taste, then serve the stew with the lamb chops.

- FLEX THE FLAVOURS -
To jazz this up, brush both sides of the chops with mint sauce after grilling and/or scatter over some Parmesan shavings.

- *Spiced* LAMB SHANKS -
WITH CHILLI AND CORIANDER POTATOES

Lamb shanks are a great alternative to stews and casseroles when you want something that looks a bit more impressive for guests. I love this recipe as you can throw everything in the pan, pop it in the oven, and leave it to cook away while you entertain your guests.

Serves 4

Prep time: 10–15 minutes

Cooking time: 3 hours

INGREDIENTS

2 peppers, any colour, deseeded and sliced

2 tbsp olive oil

2 tbsp Middle Eastern Spice Mix (see p.134)

2 tbsp tomato purée

2 x 400g cans chopped tomatoes

250ml (9fl oz) beef, lamb, or chicken stock

4 lamb shanks

100g (3½oz) dried fruit, such as raisins, prunes, or apricots

1 tsp honey

For the spiced potatoes

5 large potatoes

2 garlic cloves, sliced

2 tsp coriander seeds, lightly crushed

1 tsp chilli flakes

2 tsp turmeric

2 tbsp olive oil

salt and freshly ground black pepper

juice of 1 lime

3 tbsp chopped herbs, such as mint, parsley, or coriander, or a mix

1 Preheat the oven to 160°C (325°F/Gas 3). Fry the peppers in the oil for a minute, then stir in the spice mix and cook for another 2 minutes. Add the tomato purée, the tomatoes, and the stock, stir well, then place the shanks in the sauce, along with the dried fruit and honey, and bring to the boil. Cover the pan with a lid, pop it in the oven, and cook for 3 hours, or until the meat is tender.

2 Place the potatoes in a large pan of boiling water. Boil for 12–15 minutes then drain and leave them to cool before cutting them into 2cm (¾in) chunks.

3 Fry the garlic, coriander seeds, chilli, and turmeric in the oil for a minute. Add the potatoes, toss them in the spicy oil, then fry them gently for 5–10 minutes, until they are tender all the way through and starting to crisp up, then season and stir through the lime juice and herbs. Serve the lamb with the spicy potatoes.

- FEED THE FREEZER -

Make a double batch and freeze one batch. Thaw in the fridge for 12 hours then simmer in a lidded pan for 40 minutes, or bake at 180°C (350°F/Gas 4) for 1 hour.

- LOVE YOUR LEFTOVERS -

Shred leftover meat into any remaining sauce. Stir through a handful of fresh or frozen peas or spinach then serve with pasta and some Parmesan shavings.

- *Baked* SPICY LAMB MEATBALLS -
WITH FETA

Serve these delicious meatballs with some shop-bought flatbreads warmed through in the oven, or make your own flatbreads using the quick recipe on page 167. This moreish dish is a perfect quick mid-week dinner that goes down a treat with the whole family.

Serves 4

Prep time: *15–20 minutes*

Cooking time: *25 minutes*

INGREDIENTS

500g (1lb 2oz) minced lamb
1 onion, very finely diced
1 tbsp Middle Eastern Spice Mix
(see p.134)
salt and freshly ground black pepper
1 tbsp olive oil
100g (3½oz) feta
small bunch of mint, chopped
hummus, to serve (optional)
flatbreads, to serve

For the sauce

½ tsp ground cumin
½ tsp ground cinnamon
1 tbsp olive oil
2 garlic cloves, sliced
1 chilli, deseeded and chopped
500ml (16fl oz) Tomato Sauce (see
p.64) or 500ml bottle passata

1 Preheat the oven to 200°C (400°F/Gas 6). Mix together the mince, onion, and spices and season with a little salt.

2 Roll the mince into golf ball-sized balls then put them in a casserole dish. Drizzle over the oil then bake the meatballs in the oven for 10 minutes, or until golden brown.

3 To make the sauce, fry the cumin and cinnamon with the oil in a saucepan for a minute before adding the garlic and chilli. Fry for about another minute, until the garlic is lightly golden, then stir in the tomato sauce or passata. Bring to the boil and cook for 5 minutes, until the sauce is reduced and thickened, then season with salt and pepper.

4 Once the meatballs are browned, take them out of the oven, pour off any excess oil and pour over the hot sauce. Crumble over the feta and bake for another 5 minutes. Take the meatballs out of the oven and sprinkle over the mint then serve with the hummus, if using, and some flatbreads on the side.

- FEED THE FREEZER -

Double the ingredients for the meatballs and freeze a batch before cooking. Thaw overnight in the fridge and cook from frozen for 20, rather than 10, minutes.

- LOVE YOUR LEFTOVERS -

Mash the meatballs into the sauce, spread on top of a rolled out disc of pizza dough (see p.238), scatter over mozzarella, and bake for 10 minutes at 220°C (425°F/Gas 7).

- BEEF CASSEROLE -
WITH ALLSPICE AND PRUNES

Time permitting, I like to brown the beef off nicely here for that lovely flavour burst, but the spices in this recipe add so much flavour that you don't need to worry about browning the meat perfectly. This is even better made a day ahead so the beef absorbs the flavours.

Serves 4

Prep time: 25 minutes

Cooking time: 2 hours 30 minutes

INGREDIENTS
750g (1lb 10oz) braising steak, cut into 2cm (¾in) chunks
2 tbsp flour
2 tbsp vegetable oil
2 tsp ground allspice
1 tsp paprika
1 tbsp tomato purée
250ml (9fl oz) red wine
8 shallots, peeled and halved lengthways
2 carrots, peeled and cut into big chunks
2 celery sticks, cut into chunks
350ml (12fl oz) beef stock
8 dried and stoned prunes, or a handful or raisins
salt and freshly ground black pepper
handful of flat-leaf parsley, to serve
mashed or boiled new potatoes and selection of greens, to serve

1 Preheat the oven to 160°C (325°F/Gas 3). Place the beef in a bowl with the flour and coat the meat in the flour all over.

2 Heat the oil in a frying pan and fry the allspice and paprika over a gentle heat for a minute then stir in the tomato purée. Add the beef, stir well, and cook for another 2 minutes.

3 Pour in the red wine, give everything another stir, and bring the liquid to a simmer. Then add the shallots, carrots, celery, beef stock, and prunes or raisins and season well with salt and pepper. Bring to the boil, cover the pan, and bake it in the oven for 2½ hours, or until the meat is tender. Scatter over the parsley and serve the casserole with some mashed or boiled new potatoes and a selection of favourite greens.

- FEED THE FREEZER -
Double the ingredients and after cooking cool one batch for the freezer. Thaw it overnight in the fridge and warm it through on the hob for 10–15 minutes.

- FLEX THE FLAVOURS -
To make this extra special, top the casserole with a dollop of crème fraîche, some chopped spring onions, and a few toasted flaked almonds.

- *Quick* BEEF STIR-FRY -

If I'm away from home working I really miss fresh, home-cooked food. This stir-fry is perfect – it's full of flavour and easy to adapt with whatever you have to hand. You can also use ready-cooked noodles – they're a cheat, but quick and tasty.

Serves 4

Prep time: 20 minutes

Cooking time: 10 minutes

INGREDIENTS

2 tbsp olive or vegetable oil

2 beef steaks (fresh or frozen and thawed), excess fat removed and thinly sliced

2 tbsp ginger, grated or chopped

2 tsp garlic, crushed or grated

2 tsp chilli, any colour, deseeded and chopped

1 tsp Indian Spice Mix (see p.134) or medium curry powder

1 red onion, sliced

2 peppers, any colour, deseeded and sliced

handful of chopped carrots, cut into thin batons

handful of green beans

1 tbsp soy sauce

2 tbsp oyster sauce

1 tsp sesame oil

To serve

4 lime wedges (fresh or frozen)

2 tbsp sesame seeds, or chopped cashew or peanuts (optional)

2 tbsp coriander, chopped

noodles or sticky rice, cooked according to the packet instructions

1 Heat half the oil in a large frying pan or wok, then fry half the steak strips quickly over a very high heat. Once they have just started to brown, take the steak strips out of the pan and set them to one side while you cook the remaining meat.

2 Add the remaining oil to the pan, followed by the ginger, garlic, and chilli and fry these for a minute before adding the spice mix or curry powder. Fry the spices for a minute then add the vegetables and cook everything for another 2 minutes before adding the soy sauce and oyster sauce. Once the sauce is bubbling, return the beef to the pan to warm it through.

3 Add the sesame oil and stir this through, then serve the stir-fry with the lime wedges, sesame seeds or nuts, if using, coriander, and the noodles or sticky rice.

- FLEX THE FLAVOURS -

Use whichever meat you have to hand for this stir-fry – chicken, lamb, or pork are all ideal.

- One-pot PORK and CIDER -

This is the easiest stew in the world – just put all the ingredients in a pot and leave it to cook! It's also versatile and can be adapted using other types of meat – chicken thighs work especially well. To get ahead, make the stew and prepare the potatoes the night before then fry the potatoes the next day.

Serves 4

Prep time: 10 minutes

Cooking time: 2–2½ hours

INGREDIENTS

1.5kg (3lb 3oz) pork shoulder steaks, any excess fat removed

500ml bottle cider

500ml (16fl oz) chicken stock

250g (9oz) chestnut mushrooms

50g (1¾oz) salted butter, softened

50g (1¾oz) plain flour

100g (3½oz) frozen peas

2 tbsp wholegrain mustard

2 tbsp crème fraîche, or a dash of double cream

For the potatoes

750g (1lb 10oz) cooked new potatoes

2 tbsp olive oil

1 tbsp chopped sage leaves

4 spring onions (fresh or frozen), chopped

salt and freshly ground black pepper

zest of ½ a lemon (optional)

1 Place the pork, cider, and stock in a pan. Cover the pan and leave it to simmer gently for 2–2½ hours, or until the pork is tender.

2 Lightly crush or break up the potatoes (this is a great job for the kids to do). Heat the oil in a large frying pan and fry the potatoes for about 5 minutes, until they are starting to turn golden brown, then add the sage and spring onions. Fry everything for a few more minutes, season well with salt and pepper, then add the lemon zest, if using.

3 Take the pork out of the pan and put it to one side. Add the mushrooms to the dish, put the lid back on, and simmer gently while you mash together the butter and flour then whisk these into the cider sauce to thicken it slightly. Stir in the peas, mustard, and crème fraîche or cream, then put the pork back in the pan to warm it through. Serve the pork with the fried potatoes.

- FEED THE FREEZER -

It's worth doubling the ingredients here to stock up. Cook the whole dish as above then freeze a batch. Thaw overnight in the fridge then heat through gently in a pan.

- LOVE YOUR LEFTOVERS -

Use up leftover sauce with pasta. Shred the meat and stir a handful of spinach into the sauce. Add cooked pasta and serve with grated Parmesan.

- *Posh* BANGERS AND BEANS -

Tinned baked beans and cheap sausages take me back to my childhood camping trips. Luckily times have changed quite a bit since then and this delicious recipe is now an on-demand weekly family supper in our household – the boys absolutely love it!

Serves 4

Prep time: 10 minutes

Cooking time: 20 minutes

INGREDIENTS

12 good-quality pork chipolatas

2 leeks, finely chopped

2 garlic cloves, sliced

2 peppers, any colour, deseeded and diced

2 tbsp olive oil

2 tsp Hot and Smoky Spice Mix (see p.134)

1 tsp vinegar, any type

1 tsp brown sugar

600ml (1 pint) Tomato Sauce (see p.64), or 2 x 400g cans chopped tomatoes

2 x 400g cans mixed beans or any tinned beans, drained and rinsed

salt and freshly ground black pepper

1 tbsp chopped chives or flat-leaf parsley, to serve

1 Preheat the grill and cook the sausages until browned, letting any excess fat drain away. Gently fry the leeks, garlic, and peppers in the oil for 5 minutes, until these are soft, then add the spice mix and cook for another 2 minutes. Stir in the vinegar and sugar then tip in the tomato sauce or tomatoes.

2 Add the beans, season with salt and pepper, then simmer the dish gently for 10 minutes. Serve the sausages alongside the beans, together with a good sprinkling of the chopped herbs.

- FLEX THE FLAVOURS -

If you have any bacon or chorizo in the fridge, cut it into small pieces and fry it with the peppers to intensify the flavour.

- LOVE YOUR LEFTOVERS -

Chill any leftover beans. For a tasty lunch, gently reheat them and serve them on toast with a fried egg, crumbled feta, coriander, and a dash of chilli sauce.

10 BATCH-COOKING AND FREEZING

Cooking in bulk to stock up the freezer with ready-made meals is one of the most efficient ways to save time in the kitchen. Follow the tips below to avoid batch-cooking pitfalls and freeze with ease.

1 Check your seasoning

Salt and chilli become stronger over time so if you are planning to freeze a batch of cooked food, be careful not to over-season the dish with these.

2 Use the food processor

If you're cooking up several batches of a favourite dish, that can mean a lot of chopping and prepping. To save time and effort, enlist the help of your food processor to chop up vegetables in bulk.

3 Undercook your veggies

When you're freezing cooked vegetables, either on their own or as part of a dish, undercook them slightly so they don't become overdone and soggy the second time they are heated. Simply blanch them briefly then freeze, or if they're part of a dish, cook them for slightly less time than instructed.

Portion it up

If you're stocking up on a dish or a favourite sauce, portion up before you freeze – it's quite a challenge to divide up a big wedge of frozen ragu or to halve a frozen lasagne for six when you want to feed just four.

Freeze in ovenproof dishes

Small ovenproof dishes are ideal for freezing dishes such as lasagnes and fish pies. Simply thaw and cook everything in the same dish.

6 Get rid of air

You don't want all your hard batch-cooking work to be put to waste by freezer "burn" – the term used for when air damages frozen food. Take time to get as much air as possible out of packaging before you freeze food.

Put a label on 9

Everything can look very similar once frozen, so use a permanent marker pen and stickers to label dishes clearly – state what they are and the date they were frozen.

Do regular clear-outs

Keep your freezer organized – try keeping a log of the contents. It's amazing what you can lose in there if you don't clear it out every so often.

Use sturdy containers 7

Avoid single-use plastics and invest in some good-quality airtight containers, which will withstand repeated freezing, for batch-cooking.

Pack it small

When you're freezing cooked ingredients in freezer bags, flatten the bags out as much as possible before freezing to reduce the space they take up in the freezer – and reduce the thawing time.

- Roasted PORK BELLY -
WITH APPLES, RED ONIONS, AND POTATOES

Pork belly is one of the cheaper cuts of meat, but it goes a long way and can be really delicious. It can be cooked quickly or long and slow. I prefer to cook it for a long time so that the fat melts away and the meat is lovely and tender – then I can enjoy time with the family while it's in the oven.

Serves 4

Prep time: 10 minutes

Cooking time: 2 hours 45 minutes

INGREDIENTS

1.5kg (3lb 3oz) pork belly, skin scored

1 tsp thyme leaves or lightly crushed fennel seeds

sea salt and freshly ground black pepper

500g (1lb 2oz) new potatoes, halved

2 red onions, peeled and each cut into 8 wedges

2 eating apples, any type, each cut into 6 wedges

a few sage leaves

green veggies, to serve

For the gravy

40g (1¼oz) butter

40g (1¼oz) flour

150ml (5fl oz) cider or white wine

200ml (7fl oz) chicken stock

1 tbsp chopped chives or parsley

1 tbsp crème fraîche (optional)

1 Preheat the oven to 200°C (400°F/Gas 6). Place the pork belly in a roasting tray, skin-side up, then sprinkle the thyme or fennel and a good pinch of salt over the skin. Roast in the oven for 45 minutes, until the skin starts to crisp up.

2 Take the pork out of oven and drain off any excess fat. Place the potatoes in the pan, season with salt and pepper, then put the pork back in, sitting it on top of the potatoes. Reduce the oven temperature to 160°C (325°F/Gas 3) and roast everything for another hour. After this time, add the onions, apples, and sage leaves and roast for a further hour, or until the pork is really tender.

3 To make the gravy, melt the butter in a pan. Stir in the flour and cook for 2 minutes then gradually whisk in the cider or wine and simmer for 2 minutes before adding the stock. Continue to simmer for 20 minutes, or until the sauce has reduced and thickened, then stir in the herbs and, if using, the crème fraîche and season to taste.

4 Remove the pork from the oven and cut it into portions then serve it with the apples, potatoes, onions, and cider gravy – oh, and lots of green veggies.

- LOVE YOUR LEFTOVERS -

Use leftover pork in my Pad Thai or Cha Han (see pages 62 and 70), or make Singapore noodles: remove the crackling and cut up the meat finely. Stir-fry veggies and 1 tsp curry powder. Add the pork, cooked noodles, 2 tbsp oyster sauce, and soy sauce and sprinkle over finely chopped crackling.

- VENISON, APRICOT, and ALE STEW -

Venison is a delicious lean meat, but I would only recommend buying
it when it's in season – which is around July to February for red deer – as
this is when it's best value for money. If you're a bit unsure about venison,
diced leg of lamb or stewing beef works just as well here.

Serves 4

Prep time: 20 minutes

Cooking time: 2 hours 30 minutes

INGREDIENTS

750g (1lb 10oz) venison shoulder or
    leg, cut into 2–3cm (¾–1¼in) cubes
2 tbsp flour
salt and freshly ground black pepper
2 tbsp olive oil
1 onion, chopped
250ml (9fl oz) ale
2 carrots, peeled and cut into
    large chunks
2 celery sticks, cut into chunks
2 cloves
300ml (10fl oz) beef stock
75g (2½oz) dried apricots
3 sprigs of rosemary
2 tbsp redcurrant jelly
creamy mash or dauphinoise
    potatoes, to serve
green veggies, to serve

1 Place the venison in a bowl with the flour and some salt and
pepper and toss everything together. Heat the oil in a large
lidded pan and fry the venison, uncovered, until it is lightly
browned then add the onion and cook for another minute.

2 Pour in the ale, giving this a good stir, and bring to a simmer.
Add the carrots, celery, cloves, beef stock, apricots, and
rosemary, put the lid on, and simmer gently for 2½ hours, or
until the meat is lovely and tender.

3 Once cooked, remove the cloves and stir in the redcurrant jelly
then season to taste. Serve with creamy mash or some
dauphinoise potatoes and green veggies.

- FEED THE FREEZER -
Double up the ingredients, cook
as above, then cool one batch to
freeze. Thaw in the fridge
overnight then heat through
gently on the hob.

- FLEX THE FLAVOURS -
Put leftovers in a dish, lay puff pastry
over, brush with egg wash, and bake
at 200°C (400°F/Gas 6) for 30–40
minutes, until the pie is golden.
You can also swap red wine for ale.

- DUCK *with* CHERRY *and* ORANGE SAUCE -

Duck is a delicious meat and I don't think it's used often enough, even though it's available in every supermarket now. The breast meat is quite pricey so I've chosen to use legs here. The meat is really tender – you can prep it then simply slow-cook it in the oven so all the hard work is done for you.

Serves 4

Prep time: 20 minutes

Cooking time: 1 hour 15 minutes

INGREDIENTS

4 duck legs

a few sprigs of thyme

2 garlic cloves, skin on, but lightly crushed

salt and freshly ground black pepper

½ tsp Chinese five-spice (optional)

green vegetables and potatoes, to serve

For the sauce

1 tbsp olive oil

1 shallot, or 2 tbsp chopped onion

3½ tbsp port

150ml (5fl oz) fresh orange juice from 2 large oranges

1 tbsp cherry or redcurrant jam (optional)

zest of ½ an orange

100g (3½oz) frozen pitted cherries or tinned cherries

1 Preheat the oven to 180°C (350°F/Gas 4). Place the duck legs in a roasting tray with the thyme and the garlic. Sprinkle a pinch of salt and, if using, the Chinese five-spice over the skin then roast it in the oven for 1 hour 15 minutes.

2 To make the sauce, heat the oil in a frying pan and fry the shallot or onion until soft. Pour over the port, turn up the heat, and simmer the port for a minute, or until it has reduced by half, then stir in the orange juice, the cherry or redcurrant jam, if using, the orange zest, and the cherries. Simmer everything gently for another minute – allowing the sauce to thicken slightly – then season with salt and pepper.

3 Take the duck out of the oven and leave it to rest for 10 minutes before serving it with the sauce. This dish works perfectly with any kind of potato and some green vegetables.

- FEED THE FREEZER -

It's easy to double up the sauce and freeze some for a later date to use with any meat dish. Simply thaw it in the fridge for a couple of hours, or overnight, then heat it through in a pan over a low heat.

CHICKEN

- Old-fashioned ROAST CHICKEN -

Roasted chicken is a great meal and you can use the leftovers in lots of the chicken recipes here, or just make a delicious chicken sandwich! If possible, buy free range and get a slightly bigger chicken than you think you need.

Serves 4

Prep time: 10 minutes

Cooking time: 1 hour 30 minutes, plus resting

INGREDIENTS

For the roast chicken
5cm (2in) disc flavoured butter of choice (see pp.116–17), thawed, or 30g (1oz) softened salted butter, plus a knob of butter

50g (1¾oz) Herby Breadcrumbs (see p.135) or plain breadcrumbs.

selection of chopped veg – such as carrots, onion, celery, or other wonky, slightly soft veggies

1.5kg (3lb 3oz) chicken (or 2kg/4½lb to make sure there is leftover chicken)

150ml (5fl oz) white wine

hips or savoy cabbage, chopped, to serve

For the potatoes
good pinch of sea salt

1–2 potatoes per person, Maris Piper or King Edward, peeled and cut into large chunks

1 tbsp plain flour (optional)

3½ tbsp vegetable oil or goose or duck fat

For the gravy
1 tbsp plain flour

3½ tbsp white wine

250ml (9fl oz) chicken stock (either home-made, frozen and thawed, see p.65, or use a chicken stock cube)

1 tbsp red onion marmalade or redcurrant jelly (optional)

1 tbsp chopped tarragon, dill, or parsley

1 Preheat the oven to 180°C (350°F/Gas 4). Position a shelf in the middle of the oven without any shelves above it.

2 Mash together the butter and breadcrumbs. Place the veggies in a roasting tray and put the chicken on top. Loosen the breast skin and stuff the breadcrumb mixture under it. Pour the wine into the base of the tray and place in the oven, undisturbed, for 1 hour 30 minutes – this will give you a perfectly roasted chicken. To check, pierce the thigh with a skewer to see if the juices run clear.

3 In the meantime, make the potatoes. Bring a large pan of salted water to the boil. Add the potatoes and boil for 5 minutes, or until the outsides are starting to soften. Drain, put the potatoes back in the pan, and shake it really well to fluff up the potato edges. Sprinkle over the flour, if using, and salt and shake again. Heat enough oil or fat to cover the bottom of a roasting tray. When hot add the potatoes. Gently spoon over the oil or fat to cover them then roast in the oven for 1 hour, or until golden brown and crispy.

4 Take out the tray with the chicken, lift out the chicken with tongs and put it on a dish or board to rest, covered, for 15–20 minutes.

5 For the gravy, put the tray with all the veggies on the hob. Add the flour and stir well, scraping any caramelized bits of fat from the bottom of the pan. Cook for 2 minutes, then gradually pour in the wine, stir well, and gradually add the stock.

6 Simmer gently for 10 minutes, then pass the gravy through a sieve, squashing the veggies to get lots of flavour out of them. Stir in the marmalade or jelly and herbs and season well.

7 Boil the cabbage in salty water for 4–5 minutes then drain. Put a knob of butter in the pan, then put the cabbage back in to coat with the butter before serving. Serve the chicken and gravy with the potatoes and all the veggies.

- BBQ SPATCHCOCK CHICKEN -

Spatchcocking is a great way to cut down on the cooking time of a whole chicken, plus because it's cooked on the bone it's less likely to dry out. The first time I had to prepare one was on TV (which was nerve-racking to say the least) but it's actually quite simple to do, contrary to appearances!

Serves 4

Prep time: 15 minutes

Cooking time on the barbecue: 20-25 minutes

Cooking time in the oven: 40-50 minutes

INGREDIENTS
1.5kg (3lb 3oz) free-range chicken

For the BBQ sauce
500ml (16fl oz) passata, or 400g can chopped tomatoes, blitzed in a blender until smooth
2 garlic cloves, crushed
1 tbsp paprika
4 tbsp honey
1 tbsp Worcestershire sauce
sea salt and freshly ground black pepper
¼ tsp chilli flakes

To serve
coleslaw (see p.120)
new potatoes
sweetcorn

1 Preheat the oven to 180°C (350°F/Gas 4). To make the sauce, simply pop all the ingredients in a saucepan and warm them for 5 minutes, stirring occasionally, then leave the sauce to cool.

2 To spatchcock the chicken, place the chicken, breast-side down with the legs towards you. Using kitchen scissors, cut up along each side of the "parson's nose" – the fleshy stub at the rear end of the chicken – and down either side of the back bone, cutting through the rib bones as you go. Once the back bone is free remove it (if you like, keep this to make stock). Open the chicken out like a book and turn it over then put the heel of your hand on the breastbone and flatten it, so it lies as flat as possible – and that's it!

3 Place the chicken in a large tray then pour over half the sauce. Use your hands or a brush to coat the whole chicken, taking care to get into all the corners. If you can, leave the chicken overnight or for a few hours in the fridge to take on all that flavour.

4 When ready to cook, either barbecue the chicken on a preheated barbecue for about 20 minutes, or pop the chicken in the oven for 25 minutes, then pour over the reserved marinade, using a clean basting brush to spread this over the chicken. Cook for another 5 minutes on the barbecue, or put it back in the oven and cook for another 20 minutes. Rest for 10 minutes before serving. Serve with coleslaw, new potatoes, and sweetcorn.

- FEED THE FREEZER -

Make a double batch of the BBQ sauce and freeze one batch for a later date. Simply thaw in the fridge overnight and heat through on the hob.

- LOVE YOUR LEFTOVERS -

Chill leftover chicken for up to 2 days. Warm it in a pan with any remaining sauce and add to salads or rolls, or use it in the Chicken Enchiladas on page 110.

– SPICY CHICKEN and SWEET POTATO *Curry* –

You have to love a curry, especially at the end of a long working week – maybe with a cheeky beer and a movie. This is one of my favourites because the potatoes give a natural sweetness and it's so simple to make, especially if you have a jar of my Indian Spice Mix at the ready!

Serves 4

Prep time: 15 minutes

Cooking time: 45 minutes

INGREDIENTS

1 large onion, finely chopped

30g (1oz) butter

2 tbsp oil

3 garlic cloves, crushed

5cm (2in) piece of ginger, peeled and grated

1 red chilli, deseeded and chopped

2 tbsp Indian Spice Mix (see p.134)

2 x 400g cans coconut milk

400ml (14fl oz) Tomato Sauce (see p.64), or 400g can chopped tomatoes

1 large sweet potato, peeled and cut into 1cm (½in) cubes

8 chicken thighs, skinned and boned, each piece cut into 4 pieces (or use marinated chicken from p.107)

rice, to serve

coriander leaves and toasted flaked almonds, to serve (optional)

1 Fry the onion in the butter and oil on a low heat for a few minutes, until the onion starts to turn golden brown.

2 Add the garlic, ginger, and chilli and cook for a minute before adding the spice mix. Cook for another 2 minutes, or until the spices are fragrant, then stir in the coconut milk and tomato sauce or tomatoes. Add the sweet potato and chicken and simmer gently for 40 minutes, or until the chicken is tender.

3 Serve the curry on a bed of rice, topped with the coriander and the flaked almonds, if using.

– FEED THE FREEZER –

To get ahead, make the sauce without any of the meat or vegetables and then freeze it in batches. When you want a quick curry, simply thaw the sauce in a pan over a low heat, or in the fridge overnight, then add any vegetables, meat, or fish you have to hand and simmer everything gently until cooked through.

— Baked MOROCCAN CHICKEN with COUSCOUS —

This North African dish is beautifully spiced and a favourite of mine. Baking the couscous with the main dish means you end up with a fluffy couscous topping and a crispy layer on the bottom where it has cooked in the pan. It's a one-pot wonder that saves on the washing up!

Serves 4

Prep time: 20 minutes

Cooking time: 30–40 minutes

INGREDIENTS

4 chicken breasts, skin on

2 tbsp Middle Eastern Spice Mix (see p.134) or harissa paste

2 tbsp olive oil

salt and freshly ground black pepper

400ml (14fl oz) couscous, (yes, measured in a jug!)

50 dried apricots, quartered, or dried cherries

50g (1¾oz) raisins

4 spring onions, chopped

zest and juice of 1 large orange

zest and juice of 1 lemon

400ml (14fl oz) hot chicken stock

100g (3½oz) washed spinach leaves or frozen spinach, thawed

pomegranate seeds and coriander, to garnish

8 tbsp yogurt, to serve (optional)

lemon wedges, to serve (optional)

1 Preheat the oven to 180ºC (350ºF/Gas 4). Make 3 cuts into each chicken breast, taking care not to cut all the way through.

2 Place the chicken in a bowl and sprinkle over half the spice mix then add the olive oil with a little salt. Leave the chicken to marinate for 20 minutes, or better still, overnight.

3 Put the couscous in a casserole dish and add the dried fruit, the spring onions, and the rest of the spice mix. Mix in the citrus zest and juice and pour over the stock. Season well and spread the ingredients out evenly over the base of the dish. Place the spinach on top and add the chicken breasts, skin-side up.

4 Cover with a lid and bake in the oven for 25–30 minutes, or until the chicken is cooked through. If the chicken isn't quite cooked after 30 minutes turn the fillets over, put the lid back on, and cook for another 10 minutes. Take the chicken out and set it aside to rest for 5 minutes. In the meantime, fluff up the couscous with a fork and mix the spinach through the dish.

5 Return the chicken, scatter over pomegranate seeds and coriander, and serve with yogurt and lemon wedges if you wish.

- LOVE YOUR LEFTOVERS -

Chill any leftover couscous and chicken to make a salad for tomorrow's lunch. Add torn baby gem lettuce and make a lemon and garlic dressing with 4 tbsp mayonnaise, 1 tbsp warm water, the juice and zest of a lemon, and a little chopped garlic.

- CHICKEN *Kebabs* -
WITH MINT AND YOGURT DRESSING

Everyone loves a kebab and these lightly spiced chicken ones take no time at all to prepare. They're a perfect mid-week treat but also special enough for a weekend lunch or dinner with friends – simply serve alongside a bowl of rice for a more substantial meal.

Serves 4

Prep time: 10 minutes

Cooking time: 6–8 minutes

INGREDIENTS
4 chicken breasts, skin removed, cut into long, thin strips
150ml (5fl oz) Greek yogurt
zest of 1 lemon
1 tbsp Indian Spice Mix (see p.134)
salt and freshly ground black pepper
4 small naan or flatbreads, to serve

For the mint and yogurt sauce
8 tbsp natural yogurt
1 tbsp mint jelly or mint sauce
1 small garlic clove, sliced
8cm (3¼in) piece of cucumber, grated

For the salad
250g (9oz) cherry tomatoes, halved
½ red or white onion, sliced
a few coriander and mint leaves
juice of ½ a lemon
1 tbsp olive oil
1 chilli, deseeded and sliced

1 Place the chicken in a bowl with the Greek yogurt, lemon zest, spice mix, and salt. Mix everything together and set to one side.

2 To make the sauce, mix the yogurt, mint jelly or sauce, and the garlic. Put the grated cucumber in a clean T-towel and squeeze out any excess water then add this to the yogurt, season with a little salt and pepper, and mix together well. Toss all the salad ingredients together.

3 Preheat the grill on its highest setting. Thread the chicken strips onto the skewers in a ribbon-like fashion. If you are using wooden skewers, soak these in water for 30 minutes before cooking. Place the chicken skewers on a tray, pop them under the grill, and cook for 3–4 minutes on each side, or until the chicken is cooked right through.

4 Serve the kebabs on warmed flatbreads or naan breads with the yogurt dip and tomato salad alongside.

- FEED THE FREEZER -
You can freeze the marinated chicken before cooking, which actually improves the flavour. Thaw thoroughly before cooking then grill as in step 3 above.

- LOVE YOUR LEFTOVERS -
Transform leftover chicken into coronation chicken. Cut the strips into bite-sized pieces and mix with mayo and a little mango chutney and season.

- CHICKEN *Satay* -
WITH PICKLED VEG

Most people think of chicken satay as a starter for their Thai take-away, but this easy dish can also be eaten as a curry in its own right. For a twist on this dish, try stir-frying the chicken with the unpickled veg then toss in the marinade and serve with rice noodles.

Serves 4 as a starter, 2 as a main

Prep time: 20-25 minutes, plus marinating and standing

Cooking time: 15-20 minutes

INGREDIENTS

½ tsp cumin

1 tsp turmeric

1 tsp medium curry powder

1 tbsp rapeseed or vegetable oil

2 garlic cloves, finely chopped

2 chillies, deseeded and finely chopped

5cm (2in) piece of ginger, grated

small bunch of coriander

8 tbsp crunchy peanut butter

2 tbsp soy sauce

4 spring onions, sliced

zest and juice of 2 limes

6 chicken thighs, skinned and boned, cut into 4 pieces each

400ml can coconut milk

3 tbsp dry-roasted or salted peanuts, finely chopped

sticky rice or rice noodles, to serve

1 tbsp coriander leaves, to garnish

For the pickled vegetables

1 cucumber, peeled into ribbons

2 carrots, peeled into ribbons

a few radishes, sliced (optional)

1 tbsp caster sugar

1 tbsp white wine vinegar

1 Heat a small frying pan on a medium heat and dry-fry the cumin, turmeric, and curry powder for 1 minute. Add the oil with the garlic, chillies, and ginger and fry for another minute then stir in the coriander, peanut butter, soy, spring onions, lime zest, and juice. If the marinade is a little sticky, add 150ml (5fl oz) water to loosen it up. Pour the marinade into a bowl and set it aside to cool.

2 Put 2 tablespoons of the marinade in a separate bowl, add the chicken, and stir well. Leave for 2 hours, or if possible overnight. Thread the chicken onto 4 skewers. If using wooden skewers, soak them in water for 30 minutes before cooking. If cooking on a barbecue, get this going an hour ahead of cooking. For a griddle, preheat the pan and cut the wooden skewers to fit.

3 Heat the reserved marinade in a pan with the coconut milk and simmer until thickened. Put the cucumber, carrots, and radishes, if using, in a bowl. Add the sugar and vinegar and stir. Stand for 30 minutes, or until softened, stirring occasionally. Drain any liquid.

4 Oil the chicken on both sides then lay the skewers on the medium-hot barbecue or griddle. Cook for 15–20 minutes, or until golden, turning regularly. Serve with the rest of the sauce on the side along with the vegetables, peanuts, rice, and coriander.

- FEED THE FREEZER -

Double the sauce and marinate an extra batch of chicken. Freeze in a food bag, thaw overnight in the fridge, then cook as in step 4 above.

– CHICKEN *Enchiladas* –

This great family recipe is a sure-fire winner with my kids – and me! The tortillas, the succulent, slightly spicy chicken and beans, and the tomato sauce topped with melted cheese make this a truly satisfying dish – one which I'm sure you'll be eating again and again.

Serves 4

Prep time: 30 minutes

Cooking time: 25–30 minutes

INGREDIENTS

2 tbsp rapeseed oil

6 chicken thighs, skinned and boned and cut into strips (or use leftover roast chicken)

1 red onion, sliced

2 peppers (any colour), deseeded and sliced

2 chillies (any colour, but I prefer the long green ones here), chopped

2 garlic cloves, chopped

2 tsp Hot and Smoky Spice Mix (see p.134)

600ml Tomato Sauce (see p.64), or passata, or 2 x 400g cans chopped tomatoes

400g can red kidney beans, drained

salt and freshly ground black pepper

2 tbsp coriander (optional), plus extra for scattering

10 tortillas

300g pot crème fraîche

200g (7oz) Cheddar, grated

1 Preheat the oven to 200°C (400°F/Gas 6). Heat the oil in a large frying pan over a medium heat and fry half of the chicken thighs until golden, then set these aside while you cook the remaining chicken thighs. Put the first batch of chicken back in the pan and add the onion, peppers, chillies, and garlic. Cook everything for 2 minutes, until the onion and peppers are starting to soften, then stir in the spice mix and cook for another minute until the spices are fragrant.

2 Add half of the tomato sauce or tomatoes and the kidney beans, stir through, and simmer for 5 minutes. Season with salt and pepper and stir in the coriander, if using.

3 Tip the remaining tomato sauce over the base of a 35 x 25cm (14 x 10in) baking dish. Season again with salt and pepper.

4 Lay the tortillas out on a surface and divide the chicken mixture between them, arranging it in lines down the middle of the wraps. Roll up each tortilla then place them in the dish on top of the tomato base, packing them in nice and tightly. Dot crème fraîche over the tortillas and sprinkle them with the cheese. Season again then bake in the oven for 25–30 minutes, until the top is golden and bubbling. Once cooked, take the dish out of the oven and scatter some coriander over the top.

– FEED THE FREEZER –

Make up a second batch and freeze the whole dish before baking then thaw in the fridge overnight and cook as above.

– FLEX THE FLAVOURS –

It's easy to swap the chicken for veggie alternatives such as tofu, or just pack the tortillas with lots of different vegetables!

- CHICKEN *Chasseur* -

Sometimes the "oldies" are simply the best. This is such a classic recipe and I remember my grandmother cooking it for our family get-togethers. It's easy to make but full of flavour because the chicken is cooked on the bone and there's lots of red wine in it!

Serves 4

Prep time: 15-20 minutes

Cooking time: 1 hour

INGREDIENTS

2 tbsp olive oil

8 chicken thighs, skin on, bone in, or 4 chicken legs

140g (5oz) streaky bacon, diced, or lardons

12 button onions, or 8 small shallots

250g (9oz) button or chestnut mushrooms

1 tbsp plain flour

2 tbsp tomato purée

250ml (9fl oz) red wine

500ml (16fl oz) chicken stock

a few sprigs of thyme

1 bay leaf (optional)

1 tbsp flat-leaf parsley or chives, chopped

mashed potato and green vegetables, to serve

1 Heat the oil in a casserole dish. Add the chicken thighs, skin-side down, and brown these well, then take them out of the pan and set them aside.

2 Add the bacon to the pan and cook until crispy, then add the onions or shallots and mushrooms. Fry everything for a couple of minutes then add the flour, stirring this in to coat the ingredients, and cook for another 2 minutes before adding the tomato purée and the wine, just a little at a time and stirring constantly to stop the flour going lumpy.

3 Bring the liquid to a simmer then put the chicken back in the dish and add the stock, thyme, and bay leaf, if using. Bring to the boil then half cover the dish with a lid and simmer for 1 hour, until the chicken is cooked and tender and the sauce is syrupy. Remove the bay leaf, scatter some parsley or chives over, and serve with mashed potatoes and green veggies.

- FEED THE FREEZER -

It's easy to freeze this if you want to cook a batch ahead. Cook the dish completely, as above, before freezing, then thaw in the fridge overnight and reheat through in a pan on a low heat.

- CHICKEN *Kiev* -

This classic perhaps has fallen out of favour because people think it's tricky to make; but trust me, this recipe is easy. I make Kievs in batches to freeze using different flavoured butters (see pp.116–17) – which means I do the messy prepping job just the once then enjoy Kievs straight from the freezer.

Serves 4

Prep time: 15–20 minutes

Cooking time: 15 minutes

INGREDIENTS
4 skinless chicken breasts
100g (3½oz) Garlic and Herb butter
   (see p.116)
75g (2½oz) plain flour
salt and freshly ground black pepper
2 eggs, beaten
150g (5½oz) breadcrumbs, fresh,
   frozen, or dried
rapeseed or vegetable oil
new potatoes and green salad,
   to serve

1 Preheat the oven to 180°C (350°F/Gas 4). Use a sharp knife to make a little pocket in the thickest part of the chicken breasts, taking care not to cut all the way through. Cut 2 discs from the chilled butter and pop them inside each pocket, then press down the breast to flatten and re-seal it.

2 Season the flour with salt and pepper and place the flour, beaten eggs, and breadcrumbs in separate bowls. Dip the chicken breasts first into the flour, then into the egg, and then coat them in the breadcrumbs. Dip them once more into the egg then do a final dip into the breadcrumbs so the chicken breasts are thoroughly coated in the crumbs.

3 Place the chicken breasts on a baking tray and pop them into the freezer for 10 minutes before cooking – or freeze them completely at this point for a later date.

4 Cover the bottom of a large frying pan with the oil then fry the chilled chicken for five minutes on each side, or until golden brown. Put the Kievs back on the baking tray and bake them in the oven for 15 minutes. Serve with new potatoes and a green salad.

- FEED THE FREEZER -

If you're making up a batch of Kievs, freeze the chicken on the baking tray after breadcrumbing (see above), then once frozen, transfer the individual portions into separate freezer bags so you can thaw only what you need. Thaw thoroughly before cooking and fry then bake for 15 minutes, as in step 4.

5 flavoured BUTTERS

These butters are so useful to have to hand in the freezer. Simply put the butter mixes, below, on a large double cling film sheet, roll into a sausage, freeze, then cut off discs, remove the cling film, and add straight to a recipe or thaw in the fridge as instructed.

1 Garlic and Herb

This simply flavoured butter is delicious melted over a fillet of fish, and can also be used in a whole range of dishes, including the Prawn and Summer Vegetable Risotto on page 61 or the Pea and Mint Soup with Garlic Croutons on page 168.

Mix together **250g (7oz) softened salted butter, 3 finely chopped or grated garlic cloves, 4 tbsp of chopped herbs – try parsley, chives, coriander, or rosemary, or whatever you fancy** – and **1 tbsp freshly ground black pepper**.

2 Sundried Tomato, Lemon, and Olive

This complements chicken and prawn dishes perfectly. Try it with the Chilli and Garlic Prawns on page 143, or combine with a little oil to fry prawns or chicken in.

Mix together **250g (7oz) softened salted butter** and **75g (2½oz) finely chopped sundried tomatoes**, then add the zest of **2 lemons** and **75g (2½oz) finely chopped black olives** and combine well with the butter and tomatoes.

3 Anchovy and Chilli

The more robust flavours here make this an ideal pairing for stronger flavoured meats such as lamb – use it with a little oil to fry lamb chops in, or massage it into a roast lamb before cooking. It's also great in the Prawn, Chilli, and Rocket Linguine on page 67; melted over roasted peppers stuffed with cherry tomatoes; or simply stirred through some warm pasta.

Mix together **250g unsalted, softened butter, 100g (3½oz) finely chopped anchovy fillets in oil,** the zest of **1 lemon**, and **1 tsp chilli flakes** or **1 tbsp freshly chopped chilli** – depending on how hot you would like your butter to be.

Horseradish and Chive

4

The sharpness of the horseradish works perfectly melted over steak or served with a salmon fillet for a nice flavour contrast. You can also use this in the Chicken Kiev recipe on page 114 to add a bit of a kick.

Mix together **250g (7oz) unsalted softened butter, 4tbsp hot horseradish sauce**, and **2 tbsp chopped chives**, until the ingredients are well combined.

Chilli and Coriander

5

Try melting this butter over prawn dishes, or use it in the Old-fashioned Roast Chicken on page 100.

Mix together **250g (7oz) unsalted softened butter**, the **zest of 2 limes, 3 tbsp chopped coriander**, and **1 deseeded and chopped red chilli**, combining everything well.

- CHICKEN *Pie* -

Everybody loves a pie! The best thing about this one is that you can make and serve it in the same pan, so there's hardly any washing up. Also the filo pastry is lighter than a buttery puff or shortcrust pastry. To get ahead, make the filling a day in advance, then just reheat, top with the pastry, and bake.

Serves 4

Prep time: 30 minutes

Cooking time: 15 minutes

INGREDIENTS
3–4 tbsp olive oil

750g (1lb 10oz) skinless, boneless chicken thighs, cut into large chunks

30g (1oz) butter

3 leeks, or 1 large onion, sliced

1 red pepper, deseeded and finely sliced

1 tbsp fresh thyme leaves

30g (1oz) plain flour

175ml (6fl oz) milk

150ml (5fl oz) chicken stock

100g (3½oz) frozen peas

195g can, or half a can if already opened, of sweetcorn, drained

zest of 1 lemon

salt and freshly ground black pepper

5 sheets of filo pastry

50g (1¾oz) butter, melted

1 Preheat the oven to 180°C (350°F/Gas 4). Heat some of the oil in a frying pan and add the chicken in batches, frying the thighs until they're a light golden brown. Take them out of the pan and set them to one side before repeating with the remaining thighs.

2 Add a little more oil and the butter to the pan and fry the leeks or onion, pepper, and thyme for about 5 minutes until soft. Stir in the flour and cook for another 2 minutes before reducing the heat and gradually adding the milk, stirring all the time to prevent lumps. Once all the milk is added, pour in the stock and stir well. Bring to a simmer and continue stirring until the sauce has thickened.

3 Return the chicken to the pan and simmer everything gently for 15 minutes, then stir in the peas, sweetcorn, and lemon zest and season to taste. Either transfer the mixture to an ovenproof pie dish, or if the frying pan has a heatproof handle – about 28cm (11in) in length – keep the mixture in the pan.

4 Brush one side of the filo pastry sheets with the melted butter then scrunch them on top of the pie mixture. Sprinkle a little black pepper over the top and pop the pie in the oven for 15 minutes, until golden brown and piping hot.

- LOVE YOUR LEFTOVERS -

If you don't manage to eat this pie in one go, remove the pastry top and chill the chicken filling for up to 3 days. Reheat it in a pan with 2 tablespoons of crème fraîche or cream cheese and some grated Parmesan. Add a little stock or water to loosen the mix, along with chopped herbs, then serve stirred through cooked pasta.

— Pan-fried BREADED CHICKEN —
WITH COLESLAW

Coleslaw often features in our Friday night ritual when we open the fridge and use up any leftover veg – it doesn't matter if a carrot has gone a little bendy or the apple is a bit bruised. This chicken and coleslaw combo with sweet potato wedges is a winner.

Serves 4

Prep time: 30 minutes

Cooking time: 25–30 minutes

INGREDIENTS

4 boneless, skinless chicken breasts

50g (1¾oz) plain flour

pinch of salt

2 eggs, beaten

75g (2½oz) Herby Breadcrumbs (see p.135) or fresh or frozen breadcrumbs

2 tbsp finely grated Parmesan (optional)

4 sweet potatoes, cut into wedges

4 tbsp olive oil, plus extra for frying

1 tsp Hot and Smoky Spice Mix (see p.134)

For the slaw

3 tbsp mayonnaise

3 tbsp crème fraîche

2 tbsp wholegrain mustard

juice of 1 lemon

salt and freshly ground black pepper

2 carrots, peeled and grated

1 fennel bulb, thinly sliced (optional)

¼ red or white cabbage, shredded

8 radishes, sliced

2 shallots, thinly sliced

1 apple, thinly sliced

3 tbsp chopped herbs, such as mint, dill, or parsley

1 Preheat the oven to 190°C (375°F/Gas 5). To make the slaw, mix together the mayonnaise, crème fraîche, mustard, and lemon juice and season with salt and pepper. Stir in the shredded vegetables and the apple and herbs, combine everything well, and set to one side.

2 Use a sharp knife to cut through the thickest part of each chicken breast then open it up and flatten it slightly. Season the flour with salt then place the flour in one bowl, the eggs in another, and the breadcrumbs and Parmesan in a third bowl. Dip the chicken breasts into the flour first, then into the egg, and then finish them off in the breadcrumbs so they're nicely coated.

3 Place the sweet potato wedges in a large bowl, drizzle with the oil, and sprinkle over the spice mix. Toss everything together then spread the wedges out on a non-stick baking tray and bake in the oven for 25–30 minutes.

4 While the sweet potatoes are cooking, heat a little oil in a frying pan and fry the chicken pieces in batches on both sides, until golden brown, then place them on a baking tray. Pop the chicken in the oven for 8–10 minutes, or until cooked. Plate the chicken with the wedges and coleslaw on the side.

- FEED THE FREEZER -

I often coat 8 breasts and freeze half. You can cut them into strips before crumbing to make "nuggets" for the kids. Thaw in the fridge overnight, then cook as in step 4.

CHICKEN and CHERRY TOMATO *Tray Bake*

If you have a local butcher, ask if they have chicken mini fillets – the little fillet underneath the main chicken breast. These are slightly cheaper than regular chicken breasts and I find that they're great to cook with because they don't dry out as quickly as larger chicken breasts.

Serves 6

Prep time: 15 minutes

Cooking time: 20-25 minutes

INGREDIENTS

650g (1¼lb) chicken mini fillets

2 tsp smoked paprika

3 tbsp olive oil

1 tsp Mediterranean Herb and Spice Mix (see p.135) or dried oregano or thyme

salt and freshly ground black pepper

2 garlic cloves, sliced

1 red pepper, deseeded and sliced

1 aubergine, cut into 2cm (¾in) cubes

1 fennel bulb, sliced

400g (14oz) cherry tomatoes

handful of basil leaves

3 tbsp pesto, shop-bought or home-made Pesto (see p.65)

couscous (with optional herbs), mash, or new potatoes, to serve

dollop of crème fraîche, to serve

1 Preheat the oven to 190ºC (375ºF/Gas 5). Place the chicken in a large roasting dish, add the paprika, oil, and spice mix, season, and toss everything together so the chicken is nicely coated.

2 Add the garlic, pepper, aubergine, fennel, and cherry tomatoes. Mix all the ingredients again then pop in the oven and roast for 20–25 minutes, or until the chicken is cooked all the way through.

3 Take the chicken out of the oven, scatter over a few basil leaves, then drizzle over the pesto. Serve with some couscous (stirring in some herbs if you like), or with mash or new potatoes, and a good dollop of crème fraîche.

- FLEX THE FLAVOURS -

Instead of adding the pesto in step 3, mix up the flavours here by adding guacamole and grated cheese and some soured cream instead of the crème fraîche. Either serve with couscous, as above, or use the mixture to stuff a fajita.

FISH AND SHELLFISH

- Smoked HADDOCK RAREBIT -
WITH SPINACH AND PEAS

Fish is usually paired with quite delicate flavours, but when it's smoked it can take on something a bit stronger. This simple-to-make fish dish with mustard and Cheddar really packs a flavour punch and pairs perfectly with the refreshing spinach and peas.

Serves: 4

Prep time: 25 minutes

Cooking time: 30–35 minutes

INGREDIENTS

50g (1¾oz) butter
50g (1¾oz) plain flour
600ml (1 pint) milk
1 tsp Worcestershire sauce
100g (3½oz) strong Cheddar, coarsely grated
2 tbsp wholegrain mustard
1 tsp English mustard
2 spring onions, chopped
salt and freshly ground black pepper
4 x 250g (9oz) smoked haddock fillets, skin removed
new potatoes, to serve

For the spinach and peas

25g (scant 1oz) butter
1 tbsp olive oil
250g (9oz) baby spinach leaves
200g (7oz) frozen peas
pinch of nutmeg

1 Preheat the oven to 190°C (375°F/Gas 5). Melt the butter in a pan then add the flour and stir this in well. Cook for 2 minutes then reduce the heat and gradually stir in the milk. If the sauce starts to get lumpy, beat out the lumps with a whisk. Once all the milk is added, bring everything to a simmer, stirring constantly, and cook for another 2 minutes.

2 Take the pan off the heat and stir in the Worcestershire sauce, Cheddar, mustards, and spring onions and season with the salt and pepper.

3 Grease the bottom of an ovenproof dish. Place the fish in the dish in a single layer then pour over the sauce. Pop in the oven and bake for 20 minutes, or until the fish is cooked through – you will know it's cooked when you can flake it easily with a fork or insert a cocktail skewer with no resistance.

4 For the spinach and peas, melt the butter and oil in a frying pan over a medium heat. Add the spinach leaves and allow them to wilt then stir in the peas. Cook for 2 minutes, until any water released from the spinach evaporates. Season with a pinch of nutmeg and some salt and pepper. Serve the haddock with the spinach and peas and the new potatoes.

- FLEX THE FLAVOURS -

A smoked salmon fillet works nicely here, too, in place of the smoked haddock, while the mustard-based sauce can easily accompany some pork chops.

- FISH and CHIPS -
WITH BABY GEM AND MINTED PEAS

Everybody loves fish and chips, but they can be a bit greasy and often taste best when eating freshly caught fish by the sea. This easy mid-week version of fish and chips bakes the potato chips, so avoids all that deep-fat frying!

Serves: 4

Prep time: 25 minutes

Cooking time: 30-35 minutes

INGREDIENTS
800g (1¾lb) King Edward potatoes, scrubbed
sea salt and freshly ground black pepper
4 tbsp rapeseed oil
130g (4¾oz) plain flour, or gluten-free flour
120ml (4fl oz) chilled sparkling water
4 x 175g (6oz) skinless haddock fillets

For the Baby Gem and peas
25g (scant 1oz) butter
1 tbsp olive oil
2 Baby Gems, the very end of the stems cut off, then quartered through the core
300g (10oz) frozen peas
1 tbsp mint leaves, roughly chopped
3½ tbsp stock, any type

1 Preheat the oven to 220°C (425°F/Gas 7). Line a large baking tray with greaseproof paper. Cut the potatoes into 1cm (½in) thick slices, then into 1cm (½in) wide sticks.

2 Bring a pan of salted water to the boil. Pop the potatoes in and boil for 5 minutes, or until they are just starting to soften. Drain well then tip them out on to a clean T-towel and pat dry.

3 Tip the dried potatoes into a baking tray, drizzle over 2 tablespoons of the rapeseed oil, and season with salt and pepper. Toss everything together with your hands so that the potatoes are evenly coated in oil, then spread them out in a single layer on the tray. Bake in the oven for 30 minutes until crispy.

4 Place the flour in a large bowl and season with salt. Gradually add the sparkling water to make a batter, about the same thickness as thin yogurt.

5 Heat the remaining oil in a large frying pan. Dip both sides of the fish in the batter and once the oil is nice and hot fry the fish on one side until golden, then flip it over and cook the other side – it should take 2–3 minutes on each side, depending on how thick the fish is. Once cooked, carefully take out the fish and drain it on baking parchment.

6 For the Baby Gem and peas, heat the butter and oil in a large pan. When the oil is really hot, add the Baby Gem and fry until slightly coloured, then add the peas, mint, and the stock, simmer until the stock has evaporated, and season with salt and pepper. Serve the fish and chips alongside the Baby Gem and peas.

- Mediterranean SALMON PARCEL -
WITH DILL CRÈME FRAÎCHE

This dish is perfect for lunch with friends and it looks impressive. You can make the parcel up without the wine hours before your guests arrive. I love dishes that are shared but you can make up single parcels if you prefer with 150–200g (5½–7oz) pieces of salmon – just bake for 10–12 minutes instead.

Serves 6

Prep time: 30 minutes

Cooking time: 20 minutes

INGREDIENTS

2 bunches asparagus, about 250g (9oz) in total, if in season, or green beans

1 courgette, cut in half moons

100g (3½oz) pitted olives

2 red onions, finely sliced

2 peppers, deseeded and sliced

500g (1lb 2oz) new potatoes, boiled and chopped in half

2 tbsp Mediterranean Herb and Spice Mix (see p.135)

salt and freshly ground black pepper

2 tbsp olive oil, plus a drizzle

600g (1lb 5oz) piece of salmon, skinned and pin-boned

1 can anchovies

1 lemon, cut into 8 wedges

400g (14oz) cherry tomatoes, ideally on the vine

3½ tbsp white wine

crusty bread, to serve

For the dip

200ml (7fl oz) crème fraîche

2 tbsp chopped dill

zest of 1 lemon and juice, to taste

1 Preheat the oven to 220°C (425°F/Gas 7). Roll out 2 pieces of foil on a large baking tray so you have a big rectangle to wrap around the salmon parcel.

2 If using asparagus, break off the woody ends, cut each spear in two, then put these in a bowl. Add the courgette, olives, red onions, peppers, and new potatoes, season with the herb and spice mix and a little salt and pepper, add the olive oil, then mix everything together well.

3 Tip the veggies onto the foil, spreading them out a bit. Put the salmon on top, then the anchovies, lemon wedges, and cherry tomatoes. Drizzle over a little oil, add the wine, and season with a little black pepper. Bring the edges of the foil together to wrap around the salmon, then bake in the oven for 20 minutes.

4 For the dip, mix the crème fraîche, dill, and lemon zest and juice, to taste, then season with salt and pepper.

5 Open up the parcel at the table (mind the steam!) alongside the dip and some crusty bread and let everybody help themselves.

- FEED THE FREEZER -

When supermarkets have whole sides of salmon on offer I tend to buy more than one and pop one in the freezer with this dish in mind. Thaw overnight in the fridge then follow the recipe above.

- COD and CHORIZO -

There are two types of chorizo, one that's like salami and the other is the uncooked type that's like a regular sausage. The best one here is the uncooked type, which you can often find in butchers and well-stocked supermarkets. You can also use the cured version; it's just a little firmer to the bite.

Serves 4

Prep time: 10 minutes

Cooking time: 20 minutes

INGREDIENTS

1 tbsp rapeseed oil

1 large onion, finely chopped

1 garlic clove, sliced

2 tsp Hot and Smoky Spice Mix
(see p.134), or 2 tsp paprika and
½ tsp chilli powder

120g (4¼oz) chorizo, skinned
and sliced

3½ tbsp white wine

400ml Tomato Sauce (see p.64),
or 400g can chopped tomatoes

200ml (7fl oz) vegetable, chicken,
or fish stock

100g (3½oz) roasted red
peppers, sliced

400g can chickpeas, drained

salt and freshly ground black pepper

4 x 200g (7oz) cod fillets

50g (1¾oz) black pitted olives

1 small bunch of chopped coriander
or flat-leaf parsley

crusty bread and lemon wedges,
to serve

1 Preheat the oven to 180°C (350°F/Gas 4). Heat a large frying pan on a medium heat. Add the oil and onion and fry the onion for 2 minutes, or until soft. Next add the garlic and spice mix and stir well before adding the chorizo. Cook for another 2 minutes, until the chorizo starts to release its natural oils, then pour in the wine and simmer until the liquid is reduced by half.

2 Add the tomatoes, stock, peppers, and chickpeas and simmer everything for another 5 minutes. Either transfer the sauce to an ovenproof dish, or keep it in the frying pan if this has an ovenproof handle.

3 Season the fish and place it on top of the tomato sauce then scatter over the olives. Bake in the oven for 8–10 minutes, or until the fish is cooked through and flakes easily with a fork.

4 Remove the dish from the oven, top the fish with the coriander or parsley, and serve straight away with some crusty bread and lemon wedges on the side.

- FEED THE FREEZER -

Make an extra batch of the chorizo and tomato sauce and freeze a batch. Thaw overnight in the fridge then warm through in a pan for 10 minutes on a medium heat.

- FLEX THE FLAVOURS -

Jazz this up with posh garlic bread. Make half cuts into a baguette. Slot in discs of my Garlic and Herb Butter (see p.116). Wrap in foil. Bake for 10 minutes at 180°C (350°F/Gas 4).

Smoked SALMON and HORSERADISH FISH CAKES -

WITH GARLIC AND LEMON MAYO

Plenty of people have a jar of horseradish sauce in the fridge for a roast beef on Sunday but not so many know it's a great flavour to match with smoked fish – as this recipe demonstrates beautifully.

Serves 4

Prep time: 45 minutes, plus chilling

Cooking time: 10 minutes

INGREDIENTS

800g (1¾lb) potatoes, Maris Piper or King Edward, peeled and cut into chunks

salt and freshly ground black pepper

200g (7oz) smoked salmon, cut into pieces

200g (7oz) smoked mackerel

1 tbsp chopped dill, parsley, or chives

4 tbsp horseradish sauce

6 spring onions, chopped

zest of 1 lemon

2 eggs, beaten

40g (1¼oz) flour

100g (3½oz) breadcrumbs or toasted breadcrumbs

3 tbsp oil

green salad or rocket, to serve

For the mayonnaise

6–8 tbsp mayonnaise

1 tbsp capers (optional)

2 tbsp gherkins or cornichons, chopped (optional)

1 small garlic clove, grated or finely chopped

zest and juice of ½ lemon

1 Boil the potatoes in salted water and once tender drain them well then roughly mash them – they don't have to be smooth.

2 Place the mash in a bowl, add the salmon, and flake in the mackerel. Add the herbs, horseradish, spring onions, and lemon zest, setting aside a little zest to garnish, then season with salt and pepper. Mix everything together, taking care not to break up the mackerel too much.

3 Shape the mixture into 8 patties and, if there's time, chill them in the fridge for 20 minutes to firm them up. Mix together the ingredients for the mayonnaise and season with salt and pepper.

4 Place the egg, flour, and breadcrumbs in three bowls. Season the flour with salt and pepper and dip the patties first into the flour, then the egg, and finish off in the breadcrumbs.

5 Heat the oil in the pan and cook the patties for 5 minutes on each side. If you wish, finish them off in the oven at 180°C (350°F/Gas 4) for 10 minutes to ensure even browning all over. Serve with the mayo and salad and garnish with a little lemon zest.

- FEED THE FREEZER -

Make up a double batch and when the patties are ready, put them on a disc of baking parchment then into a freezer bag or container to freeze. Thaw for 12 hours in the fridge then cook as in step 5, above.

5 handy herb and spice MIXES

Create your own herb and spice mixes with these flavourful combos to use for the recipes in this book or to add layers of flavour to meals as you desire.

1 Middle Eastern Spice Mix

Delicately spiced Middle Eastern dishes have a unique flavour profile, combining sweetness and mild spices. Add at the start of cooking with the onions to give meat and vegetable dishes, such as Baked Spicy Lamb Meatballs (p.83) or Butternut Squash and Spinach Moroccan Casserole (p.165), a subtle, aromatic taste.

Mix together **4 tbsp smoked paprika**, **2 tsp allspice**, **2 tsp ground coriander**, and **2 tsp cinnamon**. Store in an airtight jar for up to 1 year.

2 Indian Spice Mix

This mix of classic Indian spices combines warm, peppery, and spicy flavours with sweet and nutty notes. Combine with ginger, garlic, and chilli to create a flavour base for dishes, such as Quick Beef Stir-fry (p.87) or Spicy Chicken and Sweet Potato Curry (p.102).

Mix together **2 tbsp ground coriander**, **2 tbsp ground cumin**, **1 tsp turmeric**, **2 tsp mustard seeds**, **1 tsp ground cinnamon**, and **1 tsp chilli powder or flakes**. Store in an airtight jar for up to 1 year.

3 Hot and Smoky Spice Mix

These spices add heat and pungency to dishes, giving an authentic Mexican kick. Cook with the garlic and onions at the start of a dish, or sprinkle over veggies before baking, as I've done with the sweet potato wedges on page 120.

Mix together **4 tbsp smoked paprika**, **2 tsp freshly ground black pepper**, **2 tsp garlic powder**, **1 tsp ground cumin**, and **1–2 tsp cayenne pepper**. Store in an airtight jar for up to 1 year.

Mediterranean Herb and Spice Mix

A mix of herbs and spices, this has the peppery, sweet, aromatic flavours common to Mediterranean cuisine, adding subtle flavours to fish, chicken, vegetable, and pulse dishes. Sprinkle over dishes, such as Chicken and Cherry Tomato Tray Bake (p.123), before cooking.

Mix together **2 tbsp dried oregano, 1 tsp dried thyme, 2 tsp paprika, 2 tsp crushed fennel seeds, 2 tsp garlic power,** and **½ tsp freshly ground black pepper.** Store in an airtight jar for up to 1 year.

4

Herby breadcrumbs

The herb and breadcrumb combo here is a fantastic way to create a deliciously flavourful crust or topping for meats and bakes, such as the Herb-crusted Lamb (p.75) and the Spicy Roast Veggies (p.151).

Place **8 slices of bread (stale is best), crusts on,** in a food processor and blitz. Once roughly chopped add a **bunch of parsley, a small bunch of mint, 2 tbsp rosemary leaves, 1 tbsp thyme leaves,** and the **zest of 2 lemons**. Place in a container or freezer bag and store for up to 3 days in the fridge or freeze for up to 3 months.

- *Posh* FISH FINGER SANDWICH -

Now, everyone has his or her guilty food pleasure and this would be on my list. Rather than use shop-bought fish fingers, I make my own in batches to freeze so it's just as convenient. You can customize them, too – make a chunkier fish finger for a more substantial bite or try mini versions for the kids.

Serves 2

Prep time: 20 minutes

Cooking time: 15 minutes

INGREDIENTS

40g (1¼oz) plain flour

good pinch of cayenne pepper or sweet paprika

1 egg, beaten

80g (2¾oz) breadcrumbs

250g (9oz) skinless cod, haddock, or pollock, cut into 4–6 strips

3 tbsp rapeseed oil

100g (3½oz) frozen peas

salt and freshly ground pepper

1 tbsp chopped mint

2 tbsp light mayonnaise

1 tbsp dill, chives, or parsley, chopped (optional)

1 tbsp capers or gherkins, chopped (optional)

squeeze of lemon juice

2 brioche buns, or any roll of your choice – I like brioche hot dog or burger buns

1 Baby Gem, or a handful of watercress

1 Preheat the oven to 190°C (375°F/Gas 5). Place the flour in a bowl and add the cayenne or paprika, then put the beaten egg in another bowl, and the breadcrumbs in a third bowl.

2 Dip each strip of fish in the flour, then in the egg, and finally in the breadcrumbs and lay them on a baking tray. Drizzle with 1 tablespoon of the oil and bake in the oven for 12–15 minutes, or until the breadcrumbs are golden and the fish is cooked through.

3 While the fish is cooking, boil the peas in salted water for 4 minutes then add the mint and drain. Place them back in the saucepan and use a hand-held blender (or put them in a mini food processor) to blitz them with the remaining oil, until they are as smooth as you can make them. You can also crush the peas with a fork or potato masher if you prefer. Season well with salt and pepper and set aside, keeping them warm while you make the mayo.

4 Mix the mayonnaise with the herbs and capers if using, add lemon juice to taste, and season with salt and pepper.

5 When the fish is ready, add a big spoonful of the minted peas to the bottom of the bun, top with the fish, then add some lettuce or watercress and a dollop of the mayo and the top bun.

- FEED THE FREEZER -

Increase the quantites and freeze the extra fish before cooking. You can cook the fish fingers straight from frozen – just reduce the oven temperature to 180°C (350°F/ Gas 4) and cook for 15–20 minutes.

- *Tandoori*
KING PRAWN KEBABS -
WITH SPICY RED PEPPER DIP

I love making these in the summer to cook on the barbecue. Funnily enough, like most people we don't have a tandoori oven so the barbecue is the best way to get that charring effect and smoky flavour. When sunny weather is in short supply the grill is a perfectly good alternative.

Serves 4 comfortably, 6 as a starter

Prep time: 15 minutes, plus marinating

Cooking time: 10 minutes

INGREDIENTS

2 tbsp Indian Spice Mix (see p.134) or shop-bought Indian spice mix

1 red chilli, deseeded and finely chopped

2 tbsp rapeseed or vegetable oil

pinch of salt

600g (1lb 5oz) large shell-on raw king prawns, fresh or frozen and thawed for 2 hours

coriander, to garnish

For the dip

200g jar red peppers, drained completely

1 red chilli, deseeded and roughly chopped

1 small garlic clove

1 tbsp olive oil

salt and freshly ground black pepper

1 Mix together the spice mix, chilli, and oil with a pinch of salt. Place the prawns in the marinade, mix well, cover, and leave to marinate for as long as possible – ideally overnight.

2 To make the dip, place the peppers, chilli, garlic, and oil in a blender. Blitz until smooth then season with salt and pepper.

3 Preheat the grill to a medium–high heat or fire up the barbecue. Remove the prawns from the marinade and thread each one in a straight line onto a metal skewer. Cook the prawns for 6–8 minutes, turning once, or until all the prawns have turned pink. (You can also cook them on a griddle pan on the hob if you prefer.) Serve the prawns with coriander scattered over and the red pepper dip on the side.

- FEED THE FREEZER -

Marinate a double batch of prawns to pop in the freezer for a later date. The dip also freezes really well. Simply thaw everything in the fridge for 12 hours before cooking as in step 3 above.

- Teriyaki SALMON -

This sauce has such a depth of flavour that you can coat the salmon in it and cook it straight away for a delicious meal. However, if you want to prep ahead and make the salmon even tastier, marinate it in the sauce overnight for the following day.

Serves 4

Prep time: 5 minutes, plus marinating

Cooking time: 6 minutes

INGREDIENTS

2cm (¾in) piece of fresh or frozen root ginger, peeled and grated

2 garlic cloves, peeled and finely sliced

3 tbsp soy sauce

2 tbsp sweet chilli sauce or honey

1 tsp sesame oil

zest and juice of 1 lime

4 x 150g (5½oz) salmon fillets

1 tbsp rapeseed or vegetable oil

To serve

1 tbsp sesame seeds

some chilli, deseeded and chopped, to taste

small handful of coriander

4 slices of lime

sushi or sticky rice, cooked according to the packet instructions

bok or pak choi or tenderstem broccoli

1 In a dish that is large enough to fit the salmon, mix together the ginger, garlic, soy, chilli sauce or honey, sesame oil, and the zest and juice of the lime. Place the salmon fillets in the sauce and turn them over to cover them completely. At this stage, you can cook the salmon, as below, or cover it with cling film and marinate it in the fridge for up to 24 hours.

2 Heat the oil in a frying pan over a medium heat. Take the salmon out of the marinade, letting any excess sauce drip off and keeping this to one side, then put the salmon in the pan, skin-side down.

3 Cook the salmon for 3 minutes then pour in the reserved marinade and turn the salmon over to cook for another 3–4 minutes. If the sauce becomes too thick and sticky, simply add a tablespoon of water.

4 Once cooked, sprinkle over the sesame seeds, chilli, and coriander and serve with a slice of lime, the cooked rice, and the bok or pak choi or broccoli.

- LOVE YOUR LEFTOVERS -

Transform leftovers into delicious flatbreads. Mix 1 tbsp sweet chilli sauce with 1 tbsp mayonnaise. Add lime zest and enough lime juice to loosen the sauce slightly. Warm a flatbread and top it with salad leaves, cucumber batons, radishes if you have them, and the leftover salmon, then add the dressing and a few sesame seeds.

- CHILLI and GARLIC PRAWNS -

This is a personal favourite of mine and it's a quick and delicious meal to rustle up for the family. It's great with crusty bread or spaghetti, but I must admit it's so easy to make that I sometimes have it simply as a snack on its own.

Serves 6–8 as a starter

Prep time: 5 minutes

Cooking time: 5 minutes

INGREDIENTS

3½ tbsp rapeseed or olive oil

4 garlic cloves, very finely chopped

3 tbsp flat-leaf parsley, very finely chopped

1 chilli, deseeded and finely chopped

large pinch of sea salt

600g (1lb 5oz) shelled and de-veined raw king prawns (around 24 medium-sized prawns), fresh or frozen and thawed for 2 hours

lemon wedges, to serve

crusty bread or spaghetti (optional)

1 In a large frying pan, heat the oil over a medium heat. Add the garlic, parsley, chilli, and sea salt and cook for a couple of minutes, stirring constantly, until the garlic starts to soften but isn't taking on too much colour.

2 Turn the heat up and add the prawns, frying them quickly on each side until they have turned pink and are cooked through. If using fresh prawns, cook them for 3–4 minutes, or cook frozen prawns for 6–7 minutes.

3 Carefully take the prawns out of the frying pan with a slotted spoon. Serve them straight away with some of the flavoured cooking oil drizzled over and the lemon wedges on the side. For a more substantial meal, serve with some crusty bread or stir through warm cooked pasta.

- FLEX THE FLAVOURS -

If you have one of my flavoured butters (see pp.116–17) to hand in the freezer, use this instead to cook the prawns in. Simply melt a big chunk of the butter in a frying pan with a dash of oil to stop it from burning, add the prawns, cook until pink, then serve.

"

I LOVE MAKING **SEAFOOD** **AND FISH DISHES** FOR THE FAMILY. **THE SIMPLEST** *recipes are usually* THE BEST

"

- FISH PIE -

My family loves fish pie – it's the perfect comfort food and a great way to get the kids to eat fish. You can get ahead by making this up the day before and chilling it before baking, then pop it in the oven the next day for a quick post-school supper.

Serves 6

Prep time: 1 hour

Cooking time: 35 minutes

INGREDIENTS

500g (1lb 2oz) white potatoes, ideally Maris Piper or King Edward
30g (1oz) butter
salt and freshly ground black pepper

For the filling

2 leeks, sliced
1 tbsp sunflower oil
50g (1¾oz) butter
50g (1¾oz) plain flour
600ml (1 pint) semi-skimmed milk
1 tbsp mustard (ideally wholegrain)
750g (1lb 10oz) skinned and boned fish (such as smoked haddock, cod, or salmon), fresh, or frozen and thawed, cut into 2cm (¾in) chunks
250g (9oz) spinach, fresh or frozen and thawed
green vegetables, to serve

1 Preheat the oven to 180°C (350°F/Gas 4). Place the potatoes on a baking tray and bake in the oven for 1 hour, or until soft in the centre. Once cooked, cut in half and scoop the flesh into a bowl and keep the skins in the fridge to use up any leftover pie, as shown below. (Alternatively, boil the potatoes in salted water until soft.) Mash the potatoes with the butter, season, and set aside.

2 In the meantime, make the filling by frying the leeks in the oil until soft. Add the butter then stir in the flour and cook for another couple of minutes. Gradually add the milk, stirring constantly so the sauce doesn't become lumpy, then stir in the mustard and season to taste.

3 Add all of the fish and gently stir it into the sauce. Cook for 5 minutes then spoon the mixture into a deep dish.

4 If using fresh spinach, place this in a colander and pour over boiling water until the leaves wilt, cool, then squeeze out any excess water. Scatter the spinach over the fish mixture and top with the mashed potato. Leave to cool, then either freeze, or bake in the oven for 35 minutes, until golden brown and piping hot in the middle. Serve with green vegetables.

- FEED THE FREEZER -

Double the ingredients for 2 fish pies and freeze one pre-baking. Thaw overnight in the fridge then cook as above for 35 minutes, or from frozen for 1½ hours.

- FLEX THE FLAVOURS -

Try mashed sweet potatoes for the topping instead, or a mix of the potatoes. To make this extra special, add king prawns and a handful of parsley or dill.

- LOVE YOUR LEFTOVERS -

For tomorrow's lunch, add herbs, spring onions, and a dollop of yogurt to any leftover pie. Stuff the chilled skins, dot with cheese, and bake until golden.

VEGETARIAN

- Spicy ROAST VEGGIES -

WITH MOZZARELLA AND CRUMBLE TOPPING

Adding beans to these roast veggies makes this a satisfying dish in its own right. It's also a great all-in-one side dish to serve with meat and fish dishes. You can easily swap the aubergines and chickpeas served in the lamb chop recipe on page 79 with this tasty tray of vegetables.

Serves 4

Prep time: 15–20 minutes

Cooking time: 40 minutes

INGREDIENTS

1 large aubergine, cut into 2cm (¾in) cubes

2 courgettes, cut into 2cm (¾in) cubes

2 peppers, any colour, cut into 2cm (¾in) cubes

1 red onion, cut into 8 wedges

2 garlic cloves, sliced

400g (14oz) cherry tomatoes, halved

3 tbsp olive oil, plus extra for frying and drizzling

1 tbsp Hot and Smoky Spice Mix (see p.134), or 1 tbsp smoked paprika

salt and freshly ground black pepper

3½ tbsp white wine or stock

400g can beans – mixed, borlotti, or cannellini, drained

2 balls mozzarella

2 tbsp Herby Breadcrumbs (see p.135), straight from the freezer is fine or made up fresh

a few basil leaves, to garnish

1 Preheat the oven to 190°C (375°F/Gas 5). Place the aubergine, courgettes, peppers, onion, garlic, and cherry tomatoes in a large roasting dish. Drizzle with the oil then add the spice mix and season to taste. Toss everything together then drizzle over the white wine or stock.

2 Roast in the oven for 30 minutes, turning over halfway through. After 30 minutes add the drained beans and mix these into the veggies, taking care not to break the beans up. Then tear over the mozzarella and roast everything for another 10 minutes, until the beans are warmed through.

3 Fry the breadcrumbs in a little oil until lightly golden and crispy. Sprinkle the breadcrumbs over the veggies and mozzarella, drizzle over a little olive oil, and serve with a few basil leaves scattered over the top.

- LOVE YOUR LEFTOVERS -

If there are any veggies left over, pop them in the fridge then use them to make a yummy couscous salad for the following day's lunch or light supper. Simply mix the veggies with some cooked couscous, add 1 tbsp pesto or sundried tomato paste, give everything a good toss and scatter over some Parmesan shavings.

10 *ways to* FREEZE FLAVOURS

The freezer is great for stockpiling ready-prepped flavours so you can add spiciness, sweetness, or other accents to a dish in an instant. Use these clever, simple tips and have flavour solutions immediately to hand.

1 Freeze meat ready-marinated

When a recipe calls for meat to be marinated for several hours, double up the ingredients and freeze the extra portion of marinated meat before cooking. When you want to make the recipe again, half the work will have already been done – you can simply thaw the ready-flavoured meat in the fridge, cook, and enjoy!

2 Handy wine cubes

Rather than keep unfinished bottles of wine hanging around to use in cooking, instead freeze it in ice-cube trays and just add cubes as needed during cooking.

3 Spices at the ready

If a recipe calls for half a chilli or a little freshly grated ginger, chop up the whole chilli or grate the rest of the ginger and pop the extra in an ice-cube tray. Chillies and ginger can also be frozen whole then grated into dishes from frozen – perfect for when you buy a pack but just want to use one.

4 Perfect stock

Each time you roast a chicken, put the carcass in an airtight container to freeze. When you have a couple, boil them up with a bunch of veggies for a delicious home-made chicken stock (see p.65).

5 Flavour-packed Parmesan rind

The rind of the Parmesan, which we usually throw away, is fantastic for adding a salty, nutty flavour to soups – just pop it in the freezer then simmer it straight from frozen with the other ingredients, removing it before serving.

Seeds and berries

Pomegranates are delicious – effortlessly adding a sweet succulence to dishes – but they have a lot of seeds, which easily go to waste. Use what you need then freeze the remaining seeds to sprinkle over tagines and stews straight from the freezer. And in the summer, freeze fresh berries so you can enjoy a burst of summer flavour in the winter.

6 Make herb-infused oil cubes

Make frozen flavour "cubes". Chop herbs and freeze in ice-cube trays with rapeseed oil for instant herb-infused oils. Take out as needed to stir straight into stews.

8 Freeze your own "stock" cubes

When making a home-made stock, if not using it straight away, reduce it right down for a really concentrated stock and freeze in ice-cube trays. Just add 200ml (7fl oz) hot water to re-hydrate it – a brilliant way to save freezer space but have delicious stock at the ready.

7 Batch-cook and freeze base veg flavours

If a recipe starts with frying an onion or celery, chop and cook two or three times the amount needed, then freeze the extra onion or celery in portions. Simply heat through gently from frozen then carry on with the rest of the recipe. You can easily batch cook and freeze other veg, such as carrots and parsnips, too.

9 Keep flavoursome vegetable scraps

Carrot peel, tops and tails, celery off-cuts, and other veggie scraps are all full of great flavours. Freeze them in a bag and use them for stocks (see p.65).

- BAKED FETA *with* TOMATOES *and* GARLIC TOAST -

Feta is a popular addition to salads but people don't often think about baking it. It's delicious baked and makes a very quick hot veggie lunch! This dish also makes a lovely veggie starter – simply divide up the feta and bake it in individual ovenproof dishes.

Serves 4 as a starter, 2 as a main

Prep time: 5–10 minutes

Cooking time: 20 minutes

INGREDIENTS

200g block of feta

1 tbsp dried or fresh oregano

1 tsp chilli, deseeded and chopped (optional)

2 garlic cloves, sliced, plus an extra clove for the toast

200g (7oz) cherry tomatoes – red, yellow, or baby plum, halved

4 tbsp olive oil, plus 1 tbsp for the bread

4 slices of good-quality rustic bread

2 tbsp good-quality balsamic vinegar

basil (optional)

1 Preheat the oven to 200°C (400°F/Gas 6). Place the feta in a baking dish and sprinkle over the oregano, chilli, if using, and the garlic. Arrange the tomatoes around the feta then drizzle the olive oil over the cheese and the tomatoes. Cover with foil and bake in the oven for 20 minutes.

2 Brush or drizzle both sides of the bread with oil then place the slices on a baking tray. Bake in the oven for 5 minutes, until the bread is starting to crisp up, then take it out of the oven and rub the garlic clove over one side.

3 Take the cheese and tomatoes out of the oven and drizzle the balsamic over the tomatoes. Serve the cheese and tomatoes with basil leaves, if you have some to hand, and the garlic toast.

- FLEX THE FLAVOURS -

Add complexity by drizzling over some pesto – home-made (see p.65) or shop-bought – in step 3 in place of the balsamic, to give the dish a nuttier, sweet, and slightly intense flavour.

Warm HONEY-ROAST PARSNIP AND BEETROOT Salad

Not all salads have to be cold. I serve this delicious warm root vegetable salad with a bunch of watercress and a tangy lemon dressing. It makes a great side dish with meat or fish, or a delicious lunch with crusty bread. The slightly sweet dressing is a good way to entice the kids to eat root veg.

Serves 4

Prep time: 10 minutes

Cooking time: 35 minutes

INGREDIENTS

4 parsnips, peeled and cut into thin matchsticks

2 red onions, peeled and cut into wedges

2 tbsp olive oil

3 garlic cloves, lightly crushed

a few sprigs of rosemary

salt and freshly ground black pepper

4 small cooked beetroot, cut into wedges

2 tbsp honey

1 tbsp wholegrain mustard

2 large handfuls of watercress, to serve

For the dressing

4 tbsp crème fraîche

zest of 1 lemon and a little juice

1 tbsp dill or parsley, chopped

1 Preheat the oven to 180°C (350°F/Gas 4). Place the parsnips and onions in a roasting tray then drizzle over the olive oil and add the garlic and rosemary. Season well and toss everything together.

2 Roast in the oven for 25 minutes then take the tray out of the oven and add the beetroot, honey, and mustard. Give everything a good mix and pop the vegetables back in the oven for another 10 minutes then take them out and leave to cool slightly.

3 Mix the crème fraîche and lemon zest and juice together, add the herbs, and season with salt and pepper. Divide the warm vegetables between 4 plates, then top with a pile of watercress and drizzle over the crème fraîche dressing to serve.

- FLEX THE FLAVOURS -

Base this dish around carrots instead of parsnips if you prefer. And try swapping in lime for the lemon in the dressing if you enjoy a slightly more tangy flavour kick.

- COURGETTE AND SPRING ONION *Fritters* -

If you have a vegetable patch you'll know that once the courgettes start ripening, they all come at once. When there's a glut of courgettes they're great value for money – and these tasty fritters are the perfect way to use them all up.

Make 16 fritters: Serves 2 as a main, 4 as a starter

Prep time: 15 minutes

Cooking time: 25 minutes

INGREDIENTS

2 courgettes
40g (1¼oz) plain flour
½ tsp chilli flakes or paprika
3½ tbsp cold sparkling water or
 tap water
3 eggs, beaten
2 tbsp grated Parmesan
4 spring onions, chopped
salt and freshly ground black pepper
4 tbsp rapeseed oil
4 tbsp sweet chilli sauce
juice of 1 lime, or to taste
40g (1¼oz) feta
coriander or mint leaves, to serve

1 Top and tail the courgettes then coarsely grate them with a box grater. Place them in a clean T-towel and squeeze them gently in the towel so that any excess water is squeezed out.

2 In a bowl, whisk together the flour, chilli or paprika, and water. Gradually whisk in the eggs then stir in the Parmesan, courgette, and spring onions and season with salt and pepper.

3 Heat the oil in a large frying pan over a medium heat. Add spoonfuls of the mixture to the pan and fry for 3–4 minutes, or until golden brown and starting to set on top, then flip the fritters over and cook on the other side for 2 minutes. Remove from the pan and repeat with any remaining mixture.

4 Mix the sweet chilli sauce and lime juice together. Serve a stack of the fritters with some crumbled feta and a sprinkling of herbs alongside the sweet chilli and lime sauce.

- FEED THE FREEZER -

You can freeze the fritters then simply warm them through from frozen in the oven at 180°C (350°F/Gas 4) for about 10 minutes. They won't be quite as crispy, but they will still be very good.

- ONION *Bhajis* -
WITH MINT AND CORIANDER YOGURT DIP

The side-kick to a Friday night curry, the onion bhaji has always been a deep-fried affair. My version is baked and it's just as tasty, with the sweet potato adding extra flavour. You can cook these in advance then cool them and simply warm them through in a preheated oven for 10 minutes.

Makes 12

Prep time: 10 minutes

Cooking time: 35 minutes

INGREDIENTS

2 eggs, beaten

120g (4¼oz) plain flour or gluten-free chickpea gram flour

1 tsp Indian Spice Mix (see p.134) or curry powder

salt and freshly ground black pepper

1 tsp chilli, deseeded and chopped

3 onions, sliced

1 sweet potato, peeled and grated

2 tbsp vegetable oil

small handful of coriander, to serve

squeeze of lemon or lime juice, to serve

For the dip

6 tbsp thick natural yogurt

1 tbsp mint sauce or fresh mint, chopped

a little lemon or lime zest

10cm (4in) piece of cucumber, deseeded and chopped

1 Preheat the oven to 180°C (350°F/Gas 4). Mix together the eggs, flour, and spices, and add a pinch of salt, making sure everything is well combined, then stir in the chilli, onions, and sweet potato and give everything a good stir.

2 In a non-stick muffin tin, or silicone cupcake cases placed on a tray, add a drop of oil into each hole so the base is covered, then pop the tin, or cases, in the oven to heat up the oil. After 5 minutes, take the tin out and dollop a spoonful of the onion mixture into each hole, pressing it down so it is nice and compact, then bake in the oven for 30 minutes.

3 To make the dip, simply mix together the yogurt, mint, zest, and cucumber and season. Serve the onion bhajis with some coriander, a squeeze of lime or lemon, and the dip for dunking.

- FEED THE FREEZER -

Cool the bhajis and freeze them on a tray. When solid, put them in a sealed container or bag. Thaw overnight in the fridge. Heat for 10 minutes at 180°C (350°F/Gas 4).

- FLEX THE FLAVOURS -

This is a great recipe for using up those wonky veg in the back of the fridge – carrots, white potatoes, red onions, and parsnips are all brilliant sweet potato substitutes.

- SWEET POTATO *with* ROCKET *and* BLUE CHEESE -

If you're cooking this for friends or just want to get ahead for the following evening, roast the sweet potatoes and leave them to cool before popping them in the fridge. When you want to eat, simply place them back in the oven for 10 minutes, with the cheese and rocket, and they're ready to serve.

Serves 4

Prep time: 10 minutes

Cooking time: 30 minutes

INGREDIENTS

1.25kg (2¾lb) sweet potatoes, cut into rough wedges

2 tbsp olive oil

½ tsp chilli flakes

2 garlic cloves, sliced

salt and freshly ground black pepper

50g (1¾oz) rocket leaves or baby spinach

8 sage leaves

30g (1oz) pecans or 25 pine nuts

150g (5½oz) Gorgonzola or other soft blue cheese

1 Preheat the oven to 200°C (400°F/Gas 6). Place the sweet potatoes on a baking tray then drizzle them with olive oil and sprinkle over the chilli flakes and sliced garlic. Season well and toss everything together so the sweet potatoes are well coated and roast in the oven for 25 minutes, or until tender.

2 Take the tray out of the oven and scatter over the rocket leaves or spinach, sage, and pecans or pine nuts then dot the cheese over the top. Pop the tray back in the oven for another 5 minutes, until the cheese has melted, then take it out and serve the sweet potatoes as a side dish or light lunch or supper.

- LOVE YOUR LEFTOVERS -

If there is a little left over it is delicious served cold in a green salad. Or assemble leftovers on top of a flat bread and warm this through in the oven with a little more cheese on top for a quick lunchtime pizza.

- *Open* LEEK AND SAGE PIE -

The problem with traditional pies is there's just too much pastry – on the top and on the bottom – leaving little room for anything else and making them a really heavy dish. This is my way of cutting back on the pastry and upping the veg. It makes a lovely starter or lunch dish.

Serves 4

Prep time: *10–15 minutes*

Cooking time: *25 minutes*

INGREDIENTS

40g (1¼oz) butter

4 large leeks, peeled and cut into 2cm (¾in) slices

1 tbsp chopped sage

salt and freshly ground black pepper

250g tub ricotta

2 eggs, beaten, plus extra to glaze (optional)

2 tsp chilli, deseeded and chopped, or chilli flakes

2 tbsp parsley or chives, chopped

zest of 1 lemon

320g ready-rolled sheet of puff pastry

2 tbsp pine nuts

30g (1oz) Parmesan, grated, plus some shavings

green salad, to serve

1 Preheat the oven to 200°C (400°F/Gas 6) and place a large baking sheet in the oven to warm up.

2 Heat the butter in a frying pan and add the leeks. Cook over a medium heat for about 5 minutes, until they are soft and taking on a little colour, then add the sage and cook for another minute. Season well with salt and pepper and leave to cool slightly.

3 Mix the ricotta and eggs together then stir in the chilli, parsley, and lemon zest and season with salt and pepper.

4 Carefully lay the puff pastry sheet on the hot baking sheet and use a knife to make a 1cm (½in) border around the edge, taking care not to cut all the way through. With a fork, prick the pastry inside the border, making sure it has a good covering of fork marks.

5 Spread the ricotta mixture over the pastry, keeping the border clear, then spread over the leeks and finally scatter over the pine nuts and Parmesan. If you wish, brush the pastry border with a little beaten egg to give it a nice golden colour and shine.

6 Bake on a high shelf in the oven for 20 minutes, or until the pastry is golden brown. Top with a few more Parmesan shavings and serve with a green salad.

- FLEX THE FLAVOURS -

Top the pie with 100g (3½oz) blanched asparagus spears to add an additional layer of flavour.

- BUTTERNUT SQUASH *and* SPINACH *Moroccan Casserole* -

This is the perfect recipe for getting ahead - simply make up the butternut casserole the day before then gently reheat it through while you prepare the couscous. What's more, the flavours taste even better once the squash has had time to sit and absorb the spices.

Serves 4

Prep time: 10 minutes

Cooking time: 25 minutes

INGREDIENTS

1 onion, finely chopped

2 tbsp olive oil

2 garlic cloves, chopped

1½ tbsp Middle Eastern Spice Mix (see p.134)

1 large (about 850g/1lb 14oz) butternut squash (or any squash or pumpkin that is in season), peeled, deseeded and cut into 1cm (½in) cubes

400ml (14fl oz) Tomato Sauce (see p.64) or 400g can chopped tomatoes

300ml (10fl oz) vegetable or chicken stock

1 tbsp honey

200g (7oz) spinach, washed

salt and freshly ground black pepper

squeeze of lemon juice

chopped coriander, to serve

crème fraîche, to serve

For the citrus couscous

200g (7oz) couscous

30g (1oz) raisins, dried cranberries, or chopped dried apricots

juice and zest of 1 orange or lemon

400ml (14fl oz) boiling vegetable stock

2 tbsp olive oil

3 spring onions, chopped

1 Fry the onion in the olive oil for about 5 minutes until soft, then add the garlic and spice mix. Cook for another minute before adding the squash and stir well.

2 Add the tomato sauce or tomatoes, stock, and honey and simmer for 15–20 minutes, until the squash is soft.

3 To make the citrus couscous, place the couscous in a bowl then add the dried fruit and the citrus zest and juice – as well as any pulp from the orange flesh. Pour over the hot stock and cover the bowl with cling film or a plate. Leave to stand for 5 minutes then use a fork to fluff up the grains. Drizzle over the olive oil and season well then finish off by stirring in the spring onions.

4 Stir the spinach through the tagine and allow it to wilt, then season with salt and pepper and add a dash of lemon juice. Serve the tagine with the couscous, some coriander scattered over the top, and a dollop of crème fraîche.

- FEED THE FREEZER -

Make up a double batch of the casserole and pop it in the freezer after cooling. Defrost in the fridge overnight and then heat through thoroughly in a pan.

- FLEX THE FLAVOURS -

Swap in any veg here – try sweet potato, peas, carrots, or baby corn. Potato can take longer to cook so put this in first. You can also add grilled chicken with lemon juice.

- Creamy MUSHROOMS ON TOAST -

We always have mushrooms in the fridge at home. My wife is a vegetarian and mushrooms are the perfect veg for us both as they have that "meaty" texture so I don't feel I'm missing out! We often have this for breakfast but it makes a great lunch dish, too.

Serves 2

Prep time: 5 minutes

Cooking time: 5 minutes

INGREDIENTS

knob of butter

drizzle of olive oil

2 handfuls (about 250g/9oz) of sliced mixed mushrooms or simple chestnut mushrooms

1 garlic clove, finely chopped

6 asparagus spears, woody ends removed, cut into 2cm (¾in) pieces

3 tbsp crème fraîche

2 tbsp grated Parmesan, plus some shavings to garnish

a little stock (optional)

salt and freshly ground black pepper

2 pieces of sourdough toast

1 tbsp flat-leaf parsley, chopped

1 Heat a frying pan on a very high heat. Add the butter and a dash of oil then tip in the mushrooms, garlic, and asparagus and fry until these are lightly coloured.

2 Take the pan off the heat and stir in the crème fraîche and the Parmesan. Loosen with a little stock or water if needed and season well with salt and pepper.

3 Serve on hot-buttered sourdough toast and finish it off with a sprinkling of parsley and a few Parmesan shavings.

- FLEX THE FLAVOURS -

Toast Herby Breadcrumbs (see p.135) in a little butter and scatter on top for extra crunch. Or try adding a handful of fresh or frozen spinach to the mushrooms, or serve with a poached egg on top. For a non-veggie twist, serve with crispy bacon or ham.

- *Quick* FLATBREADS -

When there's no bread in the house but you want something quick
to mop up a yummy sauce or to make a quick pizza base from, this
is the recipe for you.

Makes 8

Prep time: 5 minutes

Cooking time: 15 minutes

INGREDIENTS

500g (1lb 2oz) self-raising flour, plus
  extra for dusting
1 tsp baking powder
big pinch of salt
2 tbsp olive oil

1 Place the flour, baking powder, salt, and olive oil in a bowl and add enough water to make a soft dough.

2 Divide the dough into 8 and roll each ball out on a floured surface until it is nice and thin. Heat a frying pan on a high heat and fry a flatbread with no oil until golden brown, then turn it over and cook the other side for a minute. Turn the flatbread out on to a plate and keep it warm in the oven while you cook the rest.

- FEED THE FREEZER -

Double the quantities here to make 16 dough
balls in step 2. Freeze 8 of the balls before
rolling out, wrapping each individually in cling
film. Thaw the balls at room temperature as
needed, then roll out and fry as above.

- PEA AND MINT *Soup* -
<u>WITH</u> GARLIC CROUTONS

This is the quickest soup around and uses one of my favourite freezer ingredients – peas! Frozen peas are every bit as good as, if not better than, fresh supermarket ones as pea skins quickly harden after podding, but when frozen fresh they keep all their succulence.

Serves 4

Prep time: 5 minutes

Cooking time: 15 minutes

INGREDIENTS
1 tbsp olive oil, plus an extra dash
4 spring onions (fresh or frozen)
1kg (2¼lb) frozen peas
1 litre (1¾ pints) vegetable stock
small bunch of mint leaves, or 1 tbsp
   of mint sauce or jelly
1 heaped tbsp crème fraîche
salt and freshly ground black pepper

For the garlic croutons
1–2 stale bread rolls
disc of Garlic and Herb Butter
   (see p.116)
olive oil

1 Heat the oil in a saucepan. Add the spring onions and fry for a minute until soft. Add the peas then the stock and bring everything to the boil.

2 Cook for 4 minutes then take the pan off the heat. Add the mint and the crème fraîche and, using a hand-held blender, blend everything until smooth. Season the soup with salt and pepper and add more mint if needed.

3 To make the croutons, tear the bread into small pieces. Heat the butter in a frying pan with a little olive oil, tip in the bread, and fry it until it is golden and crunchy.

4 Pour the soup into warm bowls and top it with the croutons and another dash of olive oil.

- FEED THE FREEZER -

Double the ingredients and freeze a batch to stock up. Slowly defrost the soup in a pan over a gentle heat until it is piping hot all the way through.

- FLEX THE FLAVOURS -

If you want to impress, top this soup with a few defrosted peas, a dollop of crème fraîche, and some chopped spring onions, as well as the croutons and drizzle of olive oil.

- Vegan CHILLI -

Many non-vegans think vegan food is a little dull and full of carrot sticks and raw celery but that's definitely not the case. This vegan chilli is packed with flavour and perfectly spiced – meat eaters certainly won't be left feeling hungry.

Serves 8

Prep time: 15 minutes

Cooking time: 1 hour

INGREDIENTS

2 tbsp rapeseed oil

1 onion, sliced

3 sticks of celery, diced

4 garlic cloves, chopped

2 tbsp Hot and Smoky Spice Mix (see p.134), or 1½ tsp cumin powder and 1 tsp paprika

400g can black beans

400g can kidney beans

400g can cannellini beans

3 x 400g cans chopped tomatoes

2 tbsp tomato purée

1 tbsp yeast extract (perfect but optional)

2 peppers, deseeded and sliced

1 green chilli, deseeded and chopped

juice of 1 lime

large pinch of salt

handful of coriander, leaves picked

vegan yogurt, to serve (optional)

rice, to serve

1 Heat the oil in a large saucepan on a medium heat. Add the onion and celery and fry for 8 minutes, or until brown, then add the garlic and the spice mix and fry for another minute.

2 While the onion and celery are cooking, drain and rinse the beans and put them in the saucepan along with the tomatoes, tomato purée, and the yeast extract, if using. Bring the chilli to the boil then leave it to simmer with the lid on for 40 minutes, stirring occasionally to stop it sticking to the bottom of the pan.

3 Add the peppers and the green chilli and simmer for another 20 minutes without the lid. Stir in the lime juice and season with salt. Serve with a few coriander leaves and a small spoonful of vegan yogurt, if you like, along with some rice.

- FEED THE FREEZER -

Make up the 8 portions and freeze any you don't need for a later date. Warm through in a pan on a low heat from frozen, or thaw overnight then reheat.

- LOVE YOUR LEFTOVERS -

Put leftover chilli on tortillas. Cook for 10 minutes at 180°C (350°F/ Gas 4). Serve with yogurt, guacamole, and a salsa of diced tomatoes, onion, oil, lime, and chilli.

5 ways to keep INGREDIENTS FRESH

Finding fresh vegetables rotting at the back of the fridge or fruit going mouldy in the fruit bowl is disheartening, not to mention a waste. Try these handy tips to keep your fruit and veg nice and fresh for as long as possible.

Ditch the plastic 1

Wrapping fruit and vegetables in plastic stops air circulating around them, which means they sweat and deteriorate faster. So, as far as possible, avoid buying fruit and vegetables in plastic packaging, or take it out of the plastic as soon as you get home and store them *au naturel* in the fridge.

2 Out of the fridge

Your spuds and harder root vegetables, such as parsnips and turnips, don't need to be chilled in the fridge, which is where many of us automatically store them. The ideal place to keep them is somewhere cool and dark – ideally a pantry, but if you don't have one of those to hand, any dry, dark cupboard will suffice.

Watch those bananas

Bananas release a gas called ethylene when they're ripening, which triggers other fruit and veg to ripen and spoil faster, so keep bananas out of the communal fruit bowl – unless you want to ripen fruit quickly. Keep bananas out of the fridge, too, while they're ripening as the cold not only stops them ripening but can also damage them, causing the skin to blacken.

Don't waste that avocado

If you're left with half an avocado, to stop the other half instantly turning brown, keep the stone in and squeeze over a little lemon or lime juice, then chill in the fridge.

Handle your herbs with care

Herbs, particularly ones such as parsley and coriander, are delicate. Most herbs can be kept in the fridge, but put them in some water or wrap them in a damp kitchen towel. The exception is basil, which withers very quickly when chilled and is completely ruined. Either buy a basil plant or put the basil stems in a glass of water and keep it by the windowsill.

- Twice-baked
GOAT'S CHEESE SOUFFLÉ -

Soufflés are often a cook's nemesis – they rise, they fall, they are wonky and they seldom look like the perfect ones in books, so why compete? Well, because by baking them twice, as this recipe does, you avoid them flopping – simple! Any strong cheese can be used here – try Cheddar or blue cheese if you prefer.

Makes 6–8 x 4.5cm (2in) ramekins

Prep time: 15–20 minutes

Cooking time: 25 minutes

INGREDIENTS
60g (2oz) butter
100g (3½oz) Parmesan, finely grated
50g (1¾oz) plain flour
250ml (9fl oz) milk
1 tbsp flat-leaf parsley, chopped
1 tsp wholegrain mustard or any other mustard
200g (7oz) soft-rind goat's cheese, crumbled
6 eggs, whites and yolks separated
150ml (5fl oz) double cream
salad leaves and warmed red onion marmalade, to serve (optional)

- FEED THE FREEZER -

Once cooled, in step 5, take the soufflés out of the ramekins and freeze on a tray then move to bags or airtight containers. Bake from frozen for 15 minutes.

1 Preheat the oven to 180°C (350°F/Gas 4) and boil the kettle. Melt the butter in a saucepan. Brush the insides of the ramekins with the butter then divide half the Parmesan between them, swirling the cheese so it sticks to the butter, then tapping out any excess.

2 Add the flour to the remaining butter and mix well. Cook over a low heat for 2 minutes then take the pan off the heat and stir in the milk, a little at a time to stop lumps from forming. Put the pan back on the heat and stir continuously, until the mixture bubbles. Pour the mixture into a bowl and leave it to cool for 5–10 minutes.

3 Once the mixture is cool, stir in the parsley, mustard, goat's cheese, and egg yolks. Whisk the egg whites until they form stiff peaks then add a big spoonful of the whites to the milk mixture and stir it in. Fold in the remaining egg whites.

4 Spoon the mixture into the ramekins – they will be almost full. Put them in a deep roasting tray or ovenproof dish, pour boiling water into the tray, and bake in the oven for 15 minutes.

5 Once cooked, carefully remove the tray from the oven, then take out the ramekins and leave them to cool. At this point they will drop and deflate. Once cooled, you can chill them in the fridge for up to 2 days before the second bake or freeze them (see left).

6 Take a knife and run it around the edge of each ramekin then tip the soufflés out and put them in individual serving dishes or in a large dish. Mix together the cream and three-quarters of the remaining Parmesan. Pour this over the soufflés and sprinkle with the rest of the Parmesan then bake in the oven for 10 minutes and serve straight away with the salad leaves and marmalade, if using.

SNACKS

- Baked SWEET POTATO CRISPS -

This snack is the healthy cousin of shop-bought crisps because hardly any oil is used to make them. They're also far tastier than standard crisps – the natural sweetness from the sweet potatoes makes them extremely satisfying and 100 per cent moreish!

Serves 4

Prep time: 10 minutes

Cooking time: 2 hours

INGREDIENTS

2 large sweet potatoes, scrubbed but not peeled

2 tbsp olive oil

¼ tsp cayenne, paprika, or chilli powder or flakes

good pinch of sea salt

1 Preheat the oven to 130°C (250°F/Gas ½). Using a sharp knife or mandoline, cut the sweet potatoes into very thin discs and put them in a bowl. Add the olive oil and spices and toss together, making sure all the potatoes are covered.

2 Lay the sweet potatoes out in a single layer on a couple of non-stick baking trays and bake in the oven for 2 hours, turning them halfway through, until they are crispy. Some of the sweet potatoes may feel a little soft after baking but they should crisp up once out of the oven. Sprinkle with sea salt, cool, and serve straight away or store in an airtight container for up to 3 days.

- FLEX THE FLAVOURS -

Instead of enjoying these as a snack, use them to jazz up a chicken salad. Simply toss them in the salad just before serving and eat the salad straight away to avoid the crisps becoming too soggy.

- *Roasted* CHICKPEAS -

These are a perfect vegan snack. Make up a batch and store them in an airtight container ready to satisfy hunger pangs swiftly when these strike. They're also a tasty pre-dinner nibble when friends are over – and take just moments to prepare, leaving plenty of time to chat.

Serves 4–6

Prep time: 2 minutes

Cooking time: 30–35 minutes

INGREDIENTS
400g tin chickpeas
2 tsp Hot and Smoky Spice Mix (see p.134)
1 tsp rapeseed oil
pinch of salt

1 Preheat the oven to 180°C (350°F/Gas 4). Drain and rinse the chickpeas in a colander then shake off any excess water.

2 Place the chickpeas in a bowl along with the spice mix and the oil and salt. Mix everything together really well then tip out onto a baking tray.

3 Pop the tray in the oven for 30–35 minutes, taking the tray out every 10 minutes to give it a shake. Take the chickpeas out of the oven and leave them to cool then store them in an airtight container for up to 1 week.

- FLEX THE FLAVOURS -
You can use any of the spice mixes on pages 134–35 for this chickpea treat – they all make an equally delicious snack.

- HAM and EGG BITES -

These are like little quiches, but with no pastry to encase them. Instead they have something even tastier – ham! These moreish mini bites are popular with kids and adults alike. They're super-quick to assemble – perfect for a weekend or after-school treat or as part of a kid's birthday spread.

Makes 12

Prep time: 15 minutes

Cooking time: 20 minutes

INGREDIENTS

a little oil

12 slices of ham or Parma ham

3 large tomatoes, quartered, seeds removed, and diced

75g (2½oz) cheese, grated

2 tbsp chives, chopped

9 eggs, beaten

salt and freshly ground black pepper

1 tsp chilli (optional)

1 Preheat the oven to 170°C (340°F/Gas 3½). Grease a 12-hole non-stick muffin tin with a little oil then use the ham to line the sides and bottom of each hole, making sure there are no gaps peeking through.

2 Stir the diced tomato, cheese, and chives into the eggs then season well with salt and pepper and add the chilli, if using. Pour the egg mixture into the lined muffin tin holes then bake in the oven for 15 minutes, until the egg is set but has a slight wobble in the middle.

3 Take the tin out of the oven and let the mini bites cool so that the centre of each one is set. Store them in an airtight container in the fridge for up to 3 days and either eat straight from the fridge or warm them in the oven or microwave.

- FLEX THE FLAVOURS -

Instead of using ham to line the tray, try smoked salmon. These versatile snacks also make a great dinner party starter – just serve them with some rocket and crème fraîche mixed with a little horseradish sauce and seasoned with black pepper.

"

SNACKS DEFINITELY HOLD A PLACE IN **OUR HOUSE** *and home-made* **SNACKS** ARE ALWAYS THE **TASTIEST**

"

- TORTILLA CRISPS
and selection of DIPS -

We all like to nibble on something while we're cooking supper or having a pre-dinner drink with friends. I like to make these healthier alternatives to crisps, which are just as tasty, and serve them with a selection of delicious dips. Make some or all of these dips as you prefer.

Serves 4

Prep time: 5 minutes

Cooking time: 10 minutes

INGREDIENTS
4–6 plain tortilla wraps
1 tbsp oil
good pinch of sea salt

For the sweet chilli and cream cheese
100g (3½oz) light cream cheese
3 tbsp sweet chilli sauce
juice of 1 lime
1 tbsp coriander, chopped (optional)

For the pea and mint dip
400g (14oz) peas, defrosted
100g (3½oz) natural yogurt
small bunch of mint, stalks removed
1 red chilli, deseeded and chopped
salt and freshly ground black pepper

For the red pepper hummus
400g can chickpeas, drained and rinsed
100g jar roasted red peppers, drained
1 garlic clove
juice of 1 lemon
4 tbsp olive oil, or the pepper jar oil

For the smoked salmon and dill
100g (3½oz) light soft cheese
50g (1¾oz) natural yogurt
125g (4½oz) smoked salmon
1 tbsp dill, chopped
lemon juice, to taste

1 Preheat the oven to 170°C (340°F/Gas 3½). Brush both sides of each wrap with oil then tear or cut them into crisp-sized pieces. Place them on a baking tray in a single layer, sprinkle over some salt, and bake in the oven for 10 minutes, turning them halfway through. Leave them to cool on the tray then store in an airtight container for up to 2 days.

2 For the chilli and cream cheese dip, simply mix everything together. To make the pea and mint dip, place the peas, yogurt, mint, and chilli in a blender and whizz until finely chopped then season with salt and pepper. Likewise for the red pepper hummus, blitz everything together in a food processor. If it is a little thick, add a dash of water.

3 For the smoked salmon and dill, mix the soft cheese and yogurt together. Finely chop the smoked salmon then stir this in, along with the dill. Add a little lemon juice to taste and season with salt and pepper. Serve the tortillas together with your selection of dips and start dipping!

- LOVE YOUR LEFTOVERS -
It's easy to use up leftover dips, which keep in the fridge for up to 2 days. Try stirring the sweet chilli and cream cheese dip or the pea and mint dip through warm pasta; use the salmon dip as a pâté for toast; or simply enjoy them with veggie sticks – carrots, peppers, celery – when you fancy a snack.

- *Spiced* POPCORN -

As a kid, popcorn was saved for the occasional cinema visit or as a special treat at home. It was always made on the hob, not in the microwave, so the sound of popping filled the kitchen. This is a slightly more grown-up version with a bit of heat and spice.

Makes 1 large bowlful

Prep time: 5 minutes

Cooking time: 6–8 minutes

INGREDIENTS
30g (1oz) popcorn kernels
1 tbsp oil
50g (1¾oz) butter
1 tbsp brown sugar
¼ tsp chilli powder
½ tsp cinnamon
pinch of salt

1 Heat the oil in a large lidded saucepan. Add the popcorn, then cover the pan and cook the corn for 2–3 minutes, or until the popping starts to slow down or stops.

2 Take the pan off the hob and tip the popcorn into a large bowl. Put the pan back on the heat and melt the butter and sugar together, then add the chilli, cinnamon, and salt. Cook for 1 minute then pour the butter mixture over the popcorn and give everything a good toss to coat the popcorn. Leave the popcorn to cool then serve straight away.

- FLEX THE FLAVOURS -
Any of my spice mixes on pages 134–35 will work well for savoury popcorn. Just cook the spices in the melted butter, as in step 2, for 1 minute then add to the popcorn. For a simpler flavour, add sugar and salt with the butter.

- SPICED NUTS *and* SEES -

Nuts and seeds are perfect for snacking on, and this completely moreish recipe is incredibly simple to make but much tastier than shop-bought snacks. These make a great gift, too – just pop them in an empty jam jar and put an attractive customized label on them!

Makes 500g (1lb 2oz), or about 2 jam jars' worth

Prep time: 5 minutes

Cooking time: 20 minutes, plus cooling

INGREDIENTS

400g (14oz) mixed shelled nuts, such as almonds, pecans, peanuts, walnuts, cashews, or macadamias

100g (3½oz) sunflower or pumpkin seeds

1 tbsp rosemary, chopped

1 tsp dried chilli flakes

2 tbsp runny honey

2 tbsp rapeseed or sunflower oil

good pinch of sea salt and crushed black pepper

1 Preheat the oven to 160°C (325°F/Gas 3). Place the nuts and seeds on a baking tray, add the rosemary and chilli, then drizzle over the honey and oil. Mix everything together well then pop the tray in the oven.

2 Roast for 20 minutes, giving the nuts and seeds a stir halfway through, until they are golden brown.

3 Take the tray out of the oven, season with salt and pepper, and leave the nuts and seeds to cool on the tray, stirring them occasionally so that they cool evenly and are evenly coated. Once cooled, store in an airtight container for 1–2 weeks.

- FLEX THE FLAVOURS -

It's simple to change the flavour profile here. Using another hardy herb such as thyme instead of rosemary works equally well.

- Crispy ARANCINI BALLS -

Traditionally you would fry these but I prefer to bake them in the oven. You still get a crispy coating, but without all the additional oil. Leftover cold risotto is perfect for making up arancini – just remove any large pieces of meat or fish first then start rolling that rice!

Makes about 14 balls per 250g (9oz) rice

Prep time: 20 minutes, plus chilling

Cooking time: 20 minutes

INGREDIENTS
cooked risotto rice, leftover or freshly cooked

For the stuffing
cubes of mozzarella or any other melting cheese, or 1 tsp of leftover ragu per arancini

For the coating
50–80g (1¾–2¾oz) breadcrumbs, fresh or frozen
30g (1oz) flour
salt and freshly ground pepper
1–2 eggs, beaten
a little spray of oil, or a few tbsp olive oil

1 Preheat the oven to 180ºC (350ºF/Gas 4). To make the coating, sprinkle the breadcrumbs on a tray and pop them in the oven to toast – if toasting straight from frozen it takes just a little longer. When the breadcrumbs are a light golden brown, take them out of the oven and leave them to cool.

2 Take a large tablespoon of the risotto and roll it into a ball with your hand. If you want to stuff it, flatten it out slightly then place a piece of cheese or a teaspoon of leftover ragu in the centre and cover this in the rice, rolling it into a ball once more. Set to one side and repeat with the rest of the rice. If you have time, chill the rice balls in the fridge for 20 minutes, or until needed.

3 Season the flour with salt and pepper then tip it into a bowl. Put the eggs in another bowl and the toasted breadcrumbs in a third bowl. Roll the rice balls first in the flour, then in the egg, and finally in the breadcrumbs. Place the balls on a lined baking tray and spray with the oil or drizzle with a little olive oil then bake in the oven for 20 minutes. Take the arancini out of the oven and tuck in straight away.

- FLEX THE FLAVOURS -
Try serving the arancini with some of the Tomato Sauce on page 64 – just warm the sauce through and use it as a dipping sauce for the cooked arancini balls.

- PEANUT BUTTER and BANANA OAT Bars -

Snacks for kids that aren't full of sugar but are still appealing can be difficult to find. I make up batches of these delicious peanut oat bars and pop them in the freezer so we have a ready supply – they're perfect for the walk home from school to keep the kids moving along!

Makes about 10

Prep time: 10 minutes

Cooking time: 35–40 minutes

INGREDIENTS

200g (7oz) jumbo porridge oats

120g (4¼oz) plain flour, white or wholemeal

3 tsp ground cinnamon

1 tsp baking powder

good pinch of salt

75g (2½oz) raisins

3 tbsp desiccated coconut (optional)

2 ripe bananas

2 large tbsp peanut butter or any other nut butter you have

1 egg

2 tsp vanilla extract

375ml (12½fl oz) milk – can be dairy, nut milk, soya, or coconut

3 tbsp honey

1 Preheat the oven to 180°C (350°F/Gas 4). Place the oats, flour, cinnamon, baking power, salt, raisins, and coconut in a large bowl and mix together.

2 Mash the bananas and peanut butter together then add the egg. Beat the egg into the mixture, making sure everything is well combined, then add the vanilla, milk, and honey.

3 Add the wet ingredients to the dry ones and mix together well, then pour the mixture into a lined 20cm x 20cm (8 x 8in) tin and bake in the oven for 35–40 minutes, or until a skewer comes out of the centre clean. Leave to cool in the tray then cut into bars and store in an airtight container for up to 3 days.

- FEED THE FREEZER -

Freeze the cooked bars in an airtight container, slotting greaseproof paper between them to stop them from sticking together. Thaw at room temperature then store in an airtight container for up to 3 days.

- GINGERNUT *Biscuits* -

As much as we would like to say that our kids never have anything naughty to eat, that isn't always the case. So I figure the best thing to do is to make your own sweet treats so you can control how much sugar the children are getting while still keeping them happy. These gingernuts are yummy!

Makes about 20

Prep time: 10 minutes, plus chilling time

Cooking time: 12–15 minutes

INGREDIENTS
175g (6oz) plain flour, plus a little extra flour for dusting
½ tsp bicarbonate of soda
1 tsp ground ginger
50g (1¾oz) butter, chilled
75g (2½oz) light brown sugar
zest of 1 lemon
1 tbsp golden syrup
1 small or medium egg, beaten

1 Preheat the oven to 180°C (350°F/Gas 4). Line two baking trays with greaseproof paper. Place the flour, bicarbonate, and ginger in a bowl then use your hands to rub the butter into the flour mixture until it resembles breadcrumbs.

2 Add the sugar, lemon zest, golden syrup, and egg. Mix all the ingredients together to form a smooth dough, taking care that you don't overwork it.

3 Lightly flour a work surface then roll out the dough until it is about 1cm (½in) thick. Use a round or shaped biscuit cutter to cut out the biscuits then put these on the trays and chill them in the fridge for 30 minutes.

4 Once chilled, bake in the oven for 12–15 minutes, until they are golden brown, then take them out of the oven and leave to cool for a couple of minutes on the tray before transferring them to a wire rack to cool completely. Store the gingernuts in an airtight container for up to one week.

- FEED THE FREEZER -
Make a double batch of dough, and freeze one pre-cooking. Roll it into a sausage, wrap in cling film, and freeze. Slice off discs as desired and bake as in step 4 above.

- FLEX THE FLAVOURS -
For fancy gingernuts, put chopped stem ginger on top of each biscuit pre-baking. Bear in mind that the biscuits will go soggy faster so will last for about 3 days in a container.

- FRUIT KEBABS *with* DIPS -

Getting kids to eat fruit, or to try a new type of fruit, can be a struggle sometimes. Making it fun with a selection of enticing dips is a great way to encourage them to top up their fruit quota. In fact, dips can make things more interesting for kids and adults alike!

Makes: 1 kebab per handful of fruit

Prep time: 15 minutes

Cooking time: 5 minutes (for the chocolate dip)

INGREDIENTS

a handful of mixed fruit for each person, such as mango, pineapple, watermelon, apple, banana, pear, strawberries, or any other fruit, cut up into bite-sized pieces

For the mint and passion fruit dip

small bunch of mint leaves

2 tsp sugar

2 passion fruit

lime juice, to taste

For the vanilla yogurt dip

150g (5½oz) natural yogurt

1 tbsp honey

1 tsp vanilla bean paste or extract

For the chocolate and orange dip

100g (3½oz) dark chocolate

75ml (2½fl oz) milk

1 tbsp honey

zest of 1 orange

pinch of cinnamon

1 To make the mint and passion fruit dip, crush the mint leaves with the sugar in a mortar and pestle to form a paste then mix in the passion fruit and enough lime juice to taste. For the vanilla yogurt dip, simply mix all the ingredients together.

2 To make the chocolate and orange dip, place all the ingredients in a heatproof bowl and set this over a pan of nearly simmering water. Once the chocolate has melted, give everything a gentle stir to make sure the ingredients are well combined.

3 Thread the fruit onto bamboo skewers and serve the dips in bowls alongside the fruity kebabs.

10 ingredients to FREEZE, NOT THROW

Leftover ingredients or food that we can't find an immediate use for too often end up in the bin, but plenty of items can be frozen for later use, so check this list before tipping food away – and cut back on the waste.

1 Pasta and rice

You may be surprised to know that cooked and cooled pasta and rice can be frozen (cool and freeze rice quickly as bacteria breed if left at room temperature). Spoon excess into freezer bags in portions, spreading it out as flat as possible and removing as much air as you can, and freeze. Simply blanch in boiling water to reheat until piping hot right through.

2 Overripe avocados

When an avocado turns a little too soft before you've had a chance to use it, cut it in half, remove the stone, scoop out the flesh, and freeze it. Thaw it in the fridge and use it to make a guacamole dip.

3 Extra eggs

Not sure you can use up eggs before their use-by date? Simple. Crack them and either beat the white and yolk together and freeze them whole in ice-cube trays, or separate them and freeze each white and yolk individually. Once frozen, pop them in a bag or container and label with the date. Then when a recipe asks for 4 egg whites or 2 yolks, thaw what you need overnight in the fridge and use within 24 hours.

4 Half a tube of tomato purée

If you're left with half a tube of tomato purée, dollop tablespoonfuls on a lined baking tray, freeze, and move to an airtight bag once solid. Remove dollops to add during cooking as needed – just gently thaw in the pan then stir through.

5 The end of the cheese

Resist the urge to bin that final quarter chunk of Cheddar hanging around in the back of the fridge. Instead, grate it and freeze it in an airtight container, together with a teaspoon of cornflour to stop it clumping when it thaws. Sprinkle it straight from frozen on to bakes and pizzas before cooking.

6 Too much batter?

If everyone's had their fill of pancakes before the batter is used up, cook the remaining batter, lay the extra pancakes between sheets of greaseproof paper, and freeze them. Whenever you fancy a pancake treat just warm the pancakes in the oven or the toaster straight from the freezer.

7 Roast chicken leftovers

Rather than discard the meat left on the bone at the end of a roast, carve it off, shred it, and freeze it in portions. It's perfect for adding to soups and pasta dishes – just thaw it in the fridge overnight and heat through thoroughly with the rest of the dish.

8 Not-so-fresh bread

When a loaf is slightly stale (not mouldy), use it to make my Herby Breadcrumbs on page 135 and freeze for recipes. Or slice it to toast from frozen or even use in sandwiches – it softens once defrosted.

9 Hummus to go

If you often find yourself binning half a tub of past-its-best hummus, freeze what you haven't used in portions in airtight containers. Thaw a portion overnight in the fridge whenever you fancy a dip.

10 Citrus surplus

Slice or cut into wedges leftover lemon and lime halves and freeze in airtight bags. These are perfect to drop into a gin and tonic or for when a recipe asks for "a squeeze of lemon". Freezing citrus juice is also a great way to use up tired fruit.

- BANANA *and* CHOCOLATE BREAD -

Lighter than many cakes yet completely delicious, this banana bread treat is the ideal way to use up those overripe bananas lying around in the fruit bowl. It's also one of the simplest cakes to prepare – it really is a case of having your cake and eating it!

Makes 12 slices

Prep time: 10 minutes

Cooking time: 40 minutes

INGREDIENTS

3 very ripe bananas, plus 1 extra slightly less ripe banana, if you have it

50g (1¾oz) dark chocolate chips

2 tsp cinnamon

75ml (2½fl oz) rapeseed oil

2 tsp vanilla extract

2 tbsp honey

3 eggs, beaten

250g (9oz) self-raising flour

1 Preheat the oven to 180°C (350°F/Gas 4). Line a 900g (2lb) loaf tin with greaseproof paper or baking parchment.

2 Mash the 3 bananas until they are nice and smooth then stir in the chocolate chips, cinnamon, oil, vanilla, honey, and eggs. Mix all the ingredients together well then stir in the flour. Give everything another stir to incorporate the flour then pour the mixture into the prepared tin.

3 Cut the remaining banana, if using, in half lengthways and put the two slices carefully on top of the cake. Bake in the oven for 40 minutes, or until a skewer comes out cleanly from the centre. Leave to cool slightly then take it out of the tin and put it on a cooling rack to cool completely. Serve in slices.

- FLEX THE FLAVOURS -

It's easy to swap in some different flavours here – try replacing the chocolate with nuts, seeds, or raisins to find your favourite combinations.

- CARROT CAKE *Muffins* -

These succulent and flavourful muffins are packed with carrot and apple for natural sweetness and moisture. Using wholemeal flour also helps them to fill you up for longer, making them a truly satisfying treat. Ready in no time, these muffins are an easy way to indulge the family.

Makes 12

Prep time: 10 minutes

Cooking time: 25–30 minutes

INGREDIENTS
200g (7oz) wholemeal flour
90g (3¼oz) caster or dark muscovado sugar
2 tsp baking powder
2 tsp ground cinnamon
½ tsp ground ginger
4 tbsp vegetable oil
1 egg
80ml (2¾fl oz) milk
100ml (3¼fl oz) yogurt
2 carrots, about 200g (7oz), grated
1 apple, peel left on, grated
50g (1¾oz) raisins

1 Preheat the oven to 180°C (350°F/Gas 4) and line a 12-hole muffin tin with cases.

2 Place the flour, sugar, baking powder, cinnamon, and ginger in a bowl and mix these together.

3 Whisk together the oil, egg, milk, and yogurt. Pour the wet ingredients into the dry and mix until combined. Then fold in the carrots, apple, and raisins and divide the mixture between the 12 cases. Bake in the oven for 25–30 minutes.

- FLEX THE FLAVOURS -
These muffins are easy to adapt. Try sprinkling in some orange zest in the final mix with the fruit for a lovely citrus burst. Or replace one of the carrots with a small grated courgette, or add thin pear slices in step 3 instead of the grated apple.

PUDDINGS

-Super-simple STRAWBERRY and MINT SORBET -

There's no mysterious art to making sorbets, it's just a question of freezing and blitzing your ingredients. This refreshing palate cleanser has to be one of the easiest puddings to make in the world – it has just four ingredients and one of those is water!

Serves about 6

Prep time: 5–10 mins, plus freezing

INGREDIENTS
500g (1lb 2oz) strawberries, stalks removed and cut into quarters
8 mint leaves (optional)
2 tbsp honey
about 300ml (10fl oz) water

1 Put the strawberries on a lined baking tray and freeze until solid then transfer them to a food bag.

2 Place the frozen strawberries in a food processor along with the mint leaves, honey, and half the water and blend until smooth. You may need to help it along by stopping occasionally to push the strawberries away from the sides. Add more water if the mixture is too thick and is becoming hard to blend.

3 Once all the strawberries are blitzed, place them in a container and pop them in the freezer for 15 minutes to firm the sorbet up a little, then serve it straight away or freeze for a later date. Because there is hardly any sugar in this sorbet, if you are eating it from frozen you will need to take it out about 10 minutes before serving to soften it up slightly.

- FEED THE FREEZER -
Obviously you can make up big batches of this sorbet and store it – and for an even simpler recipe, make it with shop-bought bags of frozen fruits.

- FLEX THE FLAVOURS -
Using raspberries, peaches, or mango – or a combo of these – also works beautifully.

– Instant BANANA and HONEY ICE CREAM –

We don't often have puddings in our house but sometimes you just fancy something sweet at the end of the day. To satisfy this craving, we keep a bag of frozen banana chunks in the freezer ready to make this – it's quicker than baking and a great way to use up overripe bananas.

Serves 6

Prep time: 5 minutes, plus freezing

INGREDIENTS

6 ripe bananas, peeled and cut into chunks

3 tbsp honey

3½ tbsp cow's milk or non-dairy alternative such as almond milk, or coconut cream

1 Place the chunks of banana on a baking tray lined with baking parchment and freeze for at least 4 hours. Once frozen solid, put them in an airtight container or bag in the freezer ready to use.

2 When you want quick ice cream, put the bananas in a blender along with the honey and milk. Blitz everything, stopping occasionally to push the mixture down into the centre of the bowl. If needed, allow the frozen banana to soften a little more before blitzing again for a smooth ice cream. Once smooth, serve immediately or store in a container with a lid for a later date.

– FLEX THE FLAVOURS –

This is the perfect base to add a couple of ingredients to for a special pudding. Simply pour over some melted chocolate or salted caramel sauce, or serve with a selection of summer berries.

- Microwave MOCHA PUDDINGS -

I'm not sure about you, but during my childhood a lot of food came out of our microwave at dinner time. Nowadays the microwave is used a lot less but when you want fast results, it's still your best friend. Behold, microwave mocha puddings!

Makes 4

Prep time: 5 minutes

Cooking time: 7 minutes

INGREDIENTS

50g (1¾oz) butter, plus extra for greasing
160ml (5½fl oz) milk
2 tsp instant coffee
50g (1¾oz) pitted dates, finely chopped
1 tsp bicarbonate of soda
1 tbsp self-raising flour
50g (1¾oz) icing sugar
2 tbsp cocoa powder
50g (1¾oz) ground almonds
1 egg, beaten
Instant Banana and Honey Ice cream (see opposite), or cream or crème fraîche, to serve

1 Grease four 175ml (6fl oz) ramekins or mugs (with no metal on) with butter. In a small pan, bring the milk, butter, coffee, and dates to the boil. Take these off the heat and add the bicarbonate of soda then use a fork to mash the dates up.

2 Leave the mashed dates to cool slightly and in the meantime sift the flour, icing sugar, cocoa, and almonds into a bowl. Add the milk mixture, combine everything together well, then stir in the beaten egg.

3 Pour the mixture into the prepared ramekins. Place them around the edge of the microwave turntable and cook them for 4 minutes 30 seconds on a high heat – they will still look slightly soggy in the middle but that's okay. Serve the puddings with a scoop of banana ice cream or a little cream or crème fraîche.

- FEED THE FREEZER -

To get ahead, make the mixture up and freeze it in the ramekins. Thaw them for 4 hours at room temperature, or overnight in the fridge, then cook as above.

- FLEX THE FLAVOURS -

Put a chocolate truffle or spoonful of shop-bought salted caramel sauce in each pud pre-cooking. Serve with toasted chopped nuts, ice cream, and chocolate or caramel sauce.

5 ways to USE UP FRUIT

When fruits languish in the fruit bowl past their best, don't be hasty to throw them away. There are dozens of ways to use them up, from making tangy compotes to filling the house with the scent of freshly baked banana bread.

Banana puddings

1

Bananas have a habit of ripening quickly – and once one goes they all go. But don't bin those browning bananas, there are some delicious ways to use them. Overripe bananas are extra sweet so perfect in puddings and cakes. Try the Banana and Chocolate Bread recipe on page 198, the Instant Banana and Honey Ice Cream on page 204 or the Oat and Blueberry Pancakes on page 38. Or simply peel, slice in half lengthways, drizzle over some honey, and bake in the oven at 180°C (350°F/Gas 4) for about 5 minutes, then serve with a dollop of yogurt or crème fraiche.

Summer berry super compote

2

When the fridge is groaning with summer berries that are likely to go off before you have a chance to eat them all, make a delicious red-berry compote – just put the berries in a pan with a little brown sugar and simmer on a low heat for 15–20 minutes. Put the compote in an airtight container and either freeze it, or keep it in the fridge for up to 2 weeks. Serve with pancakes, drizzle it over ice cream, or add to your morning porridge.

Fruity puds

If you have a glut of stoned fruits, such as peaches and plums, use these to rustle up the comforting Warm Winter Fruit Salad on page 28 – either enjoy this on its own, add crème fraîche or yogurt for a fruity pudding, or make a compote for yogurts and porridge.

Appetizing apples

There's no need to throw away an excess of apples – these are perfect for so many dishes, both in puddings and to add a sweet note to savoury dishes. Try the Apple Charlotte pudding on page 209; the Roasted Fruit with Crumble Topping on page 218; or the Roasted Pork Belly with Apples, Red Onions, and Potatoes on page 94. Alternatively, add apples to the tray in the last 30 minutes when roasting a joint of pork for an apple and pork tray bake; stew apples to make a sauce for pork dishes; or add a pinch of cinnamon or a little vanilla essence to stewed apples and serve with a bowl of rice pudding.

Fruit smoothies

One of the nicest, and quickest, ways to use up excess fruit is to chop it up, removing the peel or stones if necessary, tip the fruit – one type or a combo is fine – into a blender, and blitz with milk or yogurt for a delicious breakfast smoothie. Try the Oaty Banana and Strawberry Smoothie (p.31) or make your own combo.

- *Frozen* CHOCOLATE TERRINE -

This is essentially a really, really posh ice cream. It's perfect to have stored in the freezer ready for a dinner party or when a chocolate kick is needed. For something that looks so impressive it takes next to no time to make.

Makes 8–10 slices

Prep time: 15 minutes, plus freezing

INGREDIENTS

a little oil, for greasing

150g (5½oz) amaretti biscuits

2 tbsp amaretti liqueur or hot chocolate if alcohol-free is preferred

200g (7oz) dark 70 per cent cocoa chocolate

4 eggs, separated

125g (4½oz) caster sugar

300ml (10fl oz) double cream

40g (1¼oz) dark chocolate drops

raspberries and cream, to serve

1 Line a 1.5 litre (2¾ pint) loaf tin with cling film – brushing the sides of the tin with a little oil helps the cling film to stick. Put the amaretti in a bag then crush the biscuits with a rolling pin. Place the crushed biscuits in a bowl and mix in the liqueur or hot chocolate then transfer this to the prepared tin, pressing the mixture down into the bottom of the tin.

2 Melt the chocolate in a bowl set over a pan of gently simmering water. Once melted, remove from the heat and cool slightly.

3 Whisk the egg whites until they form stiff peaks. Whisk the egg yolks and sugar in a separate bowl until thick and pale, then finally whisk the cream in another bowl until it forms soft peaks.

4 Fold the chocolate into the egg-yolk mixture, then fold in the cream, and finish by folding in the egg whites and the chocolate drops. Pour the mixture over the top of the amaretti mixture. Cover the top loosely with cling film and pop in the freezer for at least 4 hours, or better still overnight.

5 Take the terrine out of the freezer 10 minutes before serving. Tip it out of the tin and use a warm knife to cut thick slices then serve with raspberries and cream.

- FLEX THE FLAVOURS -

For a slightly different taste and texture, leave out the biscuit base and add a dash of Baileys, brandy, or coffee liqueur for a grown-up dessert.

- APPLE *Charlotte* -

This is not the quickest pudding to make, but it is very easy and uses simple ingredients. Slightly stale bread is perfect, and although white is best, it can be done just as easily with brown bread. If you have time, make the apple mixture (without the egg) the day before to get ahead.

Serves 4

Prep time: 20-25 minutes,
plus cooling

Cooking time: 30 minutes

INGREDIENTS

250g (9oz) Bramley apples, peeled, cored, and cut into 1cm (½in) chunks
250g (9oz) eating apples, any type
1 tbsp caster sugar
1 tsp vanilla extract
100g (3½oz) salted butter
6 slices of bread, crusts removed
1 egg yolk
crème fraîche or cream, to serve

1 Place the apples in a pan along with the sugar, vanilla, and half of the butter. Add a tablespoon of water, then cover the pan and cook on a low heat until the apples are soft. Use a wooden spoon to beat the apples into a rough purée, leaving a few chunks for a bit of extra texture, then set aside to cool.

2 Preheat the oven to 180°C (350°F/Gas 4). Melt the remaining butter and brush both sides of each slice of bread. Cut one disc out of one of the slices and lay it in the base of a 600ml (1 pint) pudding basin. Cut the remaining bread into strips to line the sides and top of the bowl with, then first line the sides, making sure there are no gaps whatsoever, and press the bread firmly where slices overlap to seal them.

3 Beat the egg yolk into the apple mixture then spoon this into the lined pudding basin. Cover the top of the apple with the remaining bread, making sure this overlaps again so there are no gaps. Put an ovenproof plate on top of the bread then pop it in the oven for 30 minutes, or until it is golden brown and crispy. After cooking, rest the pudding for a few minutes in the basin then turn it out and serve with some crème fraîche or cream.

- FEED THE FREEZER -

Double the quantity of apple mixture in step 1. At the end of this step, freeze the extra mix for a later date. Heat through gently from frozen to use.

- FLEX THE FLAVOURS -

Pears also work very well in this recipe, but you will need to add a little lemon juice to counter the sweetness.

- Self-saucing CHOCOLATE ORANGE PUDDING -

This is not the healthiest pudding but it can be rustled up in no time and is an indulgent treat. It's wonderfully gooey and sticky with a slight zing from the orange and is completely delicious.

Serves 6–8

Prep time: 10 minutes

Cooking time: 30 minutes

INGREDIENTS

250g (9oz) self-raising flour

130g (4¾oz) light brown muscovado sugar

50g (1¾oz) cocoa powder

zest and juice of 2 oranges

100g (3½oz) good-quality chocolate, cut into chunks

3 eggs

100g (3½oz) butter, melted

100ml (3½fl oz) milk

ice cream, to serve

For the sauce

300ml (10fl oz) boiling water

30g (1oz) cocoa powder

150g (5½oz) light muscovado sugar

1 Preheat the oven to 180°C (350°F/Gas 4). Lightly grease a 2-litre ovenproof dish.

2 Sift the flour into a large bowl and add the sugar, cocoa, orange zest, and chocolate chunks. In a separate bowl, whisk together the orange juice, eggs, melted butter, and milk.

3 Pour the wet ingredients into the dry ones and mix everything together well then transfer the batter into the greased dish.

4 To make the sauce, combine the boiling water, straight from the kettle, with the cocoa and sugar. Pour this over the cake mixture then pop it in the oven. Bake for 30 minutes, or until the top is firm to the touch, then take the pudding out of the oven and serve with ice cream.

- FEED THE FREEZER -

Double the cake mix, without the sauce, and freeze a batch in an ovenproof dish. Thaw for 4 hours in the fridge, make the sauce up, pour it over, and bake as above.

- FLEX THE FLAVOURS -

Add some extra fruity flavours in step 2 – try mixing in a handful of dried sour cherries or fresh raspberries to the batter.

- COCONUT RICE *Pudding* -

I love rice pudding – hot from the oven with a skin formed on top and served with a dollop of strawberry jam for good measure. This version is a little more refined, but just as easy.

Serves 4

Prep time: 5 minutes

Cooking time: 1 hour 15 minutes

INGREDIENTS

400ml (14fl oz) coconut milk

300ml (10fl oz) milk

zest of 1 orange

1 tsp ground cinnamon

vanilla extract

2 tbsp caster sugar

150g (5½oz) pudding or
   short-grain rice

1 mango, peeled and chopped,
   or raspberries and/or strawberries,
   or fruit of your choice, to serve

1 Place the coconut milk, milk, orange zest, cinnamon, vanilla, and sugar in a saucepan. Bring to a simmer then add the rice.

2 Stir well, cover with a lid, and simmer gently, stirring every now and then, for about 1 hour 15 minutes, or until the rice is tender. Leave to cool slightly then serve with some mango or summer berries – or other fruit of your choice.

- FLEX THE FLAVOURS -

For something a little different, cool the rice then stir in 100ml (3½fl oz) double cream. Spoon into ramekins, sprinkle over demerara sugar, then use a blowtorch or grill to melt the sugar. Cool until the sugar hardens and is crunchy, then crack open like a crème brûlée to eat.

- CHOCOLATE CHERRY *Trifle* -

This is my take on Black Forest gâteau. I don't often have time to bake a cake and fill it so this cheat's version uses shop-bought cake or leftover brownies. It's a great dinner party dish. Make the mousse the day before, then take it out of the fridge 20 minutes ahead to bring it to room temperature and soften it.

Makes 4 large tumblers, or 6 smaller ones

Prep time: 15 minutes

Cooking time: 5 minutes

INGREDIENTS

200g (7oz) 70 per cent dark chocolate, reserving 2 squares for grating

3 egg whites

1 tbsp sugar

200ml (7fl oz) double cream

250g (9oz) fresh or frozen and thawed cherries, pitted and halved

1 tbsp kirsch or brandy (optional)

about 150g (5½oz) chocolate cake or chocolate brownies, cut into 1cm (½in) cubes

100ml (3½fl oz) crème fraîche

1 Place the chocolate in a bowl set over a pan of gently simmering water. Allow it to melt slowly then remove from the heat. Whisk the egg whites until they form stiff peaks, then whisk in the sugar. Whisk the cream in a separate bowl until this stiffens.

2 Once the chocolate has cooled slightly, fold in the cream followed by the egg whites. Divide the mixture between 4 larger or 6 smaller glasses. At this stage you can pop these in the fridge to chill and take them out 20 minutes before serving to finish off assembling the trifles.

3 Mix together the cherries and the booze, if using. When you are ready to serve, top the chocolate mousse with some of the cake cubes, the cherries, and a dollop of the crème fraîche and finish it all off with a cherry half and a grating of dark chocolate.

- FLEX THE FLAVOURS -

Add a little orange zest for extra zing, and/or a tablespoon of strong coffee to the melted chocolate and simply change the cherries for raspberries or strawberries – or even some orange segments if you fancy.

- Warm RUM PINEAPPLE with LIME MASCARPONE -

This delicious dessert is incredibly simple to make, but the finished result looks rather sophisticated. The perfect pudding to impress! Prep the pineapple, lemon zest, and gingernut biscuits in advance so most of the fiddly work has been done ahead.

Serves 4

Prep time: 10 minutes

Cooking time: 10 minutes

INGREDIENTS

1 pineapple

200g (7oz) mascarpone

2 tbsp icing sugar

zest and juice of 1 lime

4 gingernut biscuits (see p.192) or shop-bought gingernuts

30g (1oz) butter

2 tbsp honey

pinch of cinnamon

2 tbsp rum

1 Cut the top and bottom off the pineapple then use a breadknife to cut all the way down the sides to take off the outer skin. Cut it in half down the middle and then into quarters to give you 4 large wedges. Finally, cut each of these into 2 long wedges.

2 Mix the mascarpone, icing sugar, and the lime zest together in a bowl, add the lime juice to taste, then set to one side. Roughly crush the gingernut biscuits.

3 Heat the butter in a frying pan and once melted, add the pineapple wedges and cook for 6–8 minutes, until they're starting to caramelize. Drizzle over the honey and add the cinnamon then cook for another minute before adding the rum – take care if you are using a gas hob as the rum could alight now, which is great but not necessary.

4 Simmer for a minute or two, until the sauce becomes syrupy, then divide the pineapples up between 4 plates. Serve each with a generous spoonful of the mascarpone along with the crushed gingernut biscuits.

- FLEX THE FLAVOURS -

If rum isn't your favourite tipple, try brandy instead. Or if you would prefer to make an alcohol-free version of this pud, using apple or orange juice in place of the rum works well and lends a bit of extra sweetness.

Roasted FRUIT with CRUMBLE TOPPING

When in season there's nothing better than summer fruits such as peaches and cherries. Out of season they tend to lack flavour, even though they can be twice the price. If you have a local greengrocer ask their advice and swap in whichever stoned fruits are most seasonal.

Serves 4

Prep time: 15 minutes

Cooking time: 30 minutes

INGREDIENTS

juice and peel of 2 oranges – zest removed with a peeler

3 tbsp runny honey

seeds from 1 vanilla pod, or 1 tbsp vanilla paste

2 cinnamon sticks

sprig of rosemary

500g (1lb 2oz) stoned fruits, such as peaches, nectarines, plums, apricots, and cherries – whichever is most ripe and use one sort or a mixture

100g (3½oz) strawberries or raspberries (optional)

yogurt or ice-cream, to serve

For the crumble topping

75g (2½oz) plain flour

60g (2oz) butter, chilled

30g (1oz) nuts, such as hazelnuts, roughly chopped

30g (1oz) desiccated coconut

75g (2½oz) oats

3 tbsp brown sugar

1 Preheat the oven to 180ºC (350ºF/Gas 4). Place the orange juice and peel in a baking tray, about 20 x 30cm (8 x 12in), together with the honey, vanilla, cinnamon sticks, and rosemary.

2 Cut the fruits in half and remove the stones then place them in the tray. Roll the fruits over in the juice, pop the tray in the oven, and roast the fruits for 15–20 minutes, depending on how ripe the fruit is. If you wish, add some strawberries or raspberries in the last couple of minutes of cooking time and warm these through with the rest of the fruit.

3 To make the crumble, place the flour in a bowl and rub in the butter. Stir in the nuts, coconut, oats, and sugar. If you wish, you can freeze the crumble at this stage (see below).

4 Spread the crumble out onto a separate baking tray and bake for 15 minutes, mixing halfway through, then when the topping is golden brown, take it out of the oven and leave it to cool.

5 Remove the rosemary sprig and cinnamon sticks from the fruit and serve the fruit with the crumble topping sprinkled over and a big spoonful of yogurt or ice-cream.

- FEED THE FREEZER -

Double the ingredients. Cook the extra fruit for just 10 minutes then freeze this and the extra crumble separately. Thaw at room temperature then assemble the pudding and bake as in step 4.

"

I'M A BIG FAN OF
ADDING ZEST OR
SPICES
TO GIVE MY PUDS
a flavour kick

"

– RASPBERRY CUPCAKE *Cheesecakes* –

Half the problem with delicious desserts is the temptation to eat too much, so by making these up into individual cheesecakes that issue is soon knocked on the head – unless you eat two! Quick to make, these will swiftly disappear.

Makes 8

Prep time: 15 minutes

Cooking time: 12–15 minutes

INGREDIENTS

75g (2½oz), or about 5, digestive biscuits, or any biscuits you have in the house

40g (1¼oz) salted butter, melted

For the filling

280g (9½oz) light cream cheese

90g (3¼oz) caster sugar, plus extra for the raspberry sauce

2 tbsp plain or cornflour

1 egg, beaten

zest of 1 lemon and 1 tsp lemon juice

300g (10oz) raspberries

crème fraîche, to serve

1 Preheat the oven to 180°C (350°F/Gas 4). Line a muffin tin with 8 paper cases.

2 Either blend the biscuits in a food processor until they resemble fine breadcrumbs or place them in a food bag and bash them with a rolling pin. Place them in a bowl, add the melted butter, and mix this in well.

3 Add a tablespoon of the biscuit mix to each cupcake case and press it down – the easiest way to do this is by using the bottom of a glass.

4 Pop the muffin tin in the fridge. In a large jug or a bowl, beat the cream cheese until smooth, then add the sugar, sift in the cornflour, and mix everything well. Add the egg and the lemon zest and juice and mix until smooth. Put 2–3 raspberries in each cupcake case then pour over the cream cheese mixture (which is why this is best done in a jug).

5 Bake in the oven for 12–15 minutes, until just set but with a slight wobble in the centre. Take the cheesecakes out of the oven and leave to cool completely. Use the back of a fork to crush half of the remaining raspberries into a rough sauce, adding a little sugar if needed. Serve the cheesecakes with a dollop of crème fraîche, some of the raspberry sauce, and a few whole raspberries.

– FEED THE FREEZER –

Any uneaten cheesecakes can be popped in the freezer then simply thawed in the fridge for 6 hours, or overnight, before devouring!

– FLEX THE FLAVOURS –

Blueberries also work really well with this recipe and you can switch the lemon for orange or lime for a flavour twist if you prefer.

FEASTS

- Big BRUNCH -

We really enjoy indulging in a big family breakfast at the weekend. It's a great way to get everybody around the table before all the various activities of the day begin. This French toast brunch with delicious toppings is a real winner – the kids love choosing what to put on their slices.

FOR THE FRENCH TOAST

Serves 4

Prep time: 5 minutes

Cooking time: 8–14 minutes

INGREDIENTS

3 eggs
120ml (4fl oz) milk
1 tbsp caster sugar
4 thick slices of bread, such as a
    farmhouse loaf, or brioche
2 tbsp unsalted butter or rapeseed oil

1 Beat the eggs and milk together, add the sugar, then pour the mixture into a shallow tray or dish and dip the bread into it, turning it over and giving it a minute or so to soak up the mixture. Repeat with all the slices.

2 Heat the butter or oil in a large frying pan then fry the soaked bread for about 2–3 minutes each side, until it is golden brown; cook the bread in batches if necessary. Serve the bread with the crispy bacon, blueberry compote, and fig and almonds and let everyone pick and choose their toppings.

FOR THE CRISPY BACON TOPPING

Serves 4

Prep time: 2 minutes

Cooking time: 7–10 minutes

INGREDIENTS

12 rashers of streaky bacon
Maple syrup

1 Grill the bacon for 7–10 minutes, until it is really crispy.

2 Serve the bacon as a topping for the French toast with the maple syrup alongside to drizzle over.

FOR THE QUICK BLUEBERRY COMPOTE TOPPING

Serves 4

Prep time: 1 minute

Cooking time: 5–10 minutes, depending on how thick you want the compote

INGREDIENTS

350g pack frozen blueberries or
   350g (12oz) fresh blueberries with
   1 tbsp water
1 tbsp honey
zest of ½ lemon
1 tsp vanilla extract

1 Place all the ingredients in a pan and warm them through for about 5 minutes, or until the blueberries start to burst.

2 Remove the cooked blueberries from the heat and serve as a topping for the French toast.

FOR THE ROASTED FIG AND ALMOND TOPPING

Serves 4

Prep time: 4 minutes

Cooking time: 10 minutes

INGREDIENTS

4 figs, halved
½ tsp ground cinnamon
1 tbsp honey
zest and juice of 1 small orange
natural yogurt, to serve
2 tbsp toasted flaked almonds

1 Preheat the oven to 180°C (350°F/Gas 4). Place the figs in a snug roasting dish and sprinkle over the cinnamon. Drizzle over the honey and add the orange zest and juice.

2 Place in the oven and roast for 5–10 minutes, or until the figs start to release their juices, which will depend on how ripe they are. Place the figs in a bowl and serve with yogurt and some toasted flaked almonds as toppings for the toast.

- MEXICAN *Feast* -

This Mexican feast has something for everyone. Serve the chilli in the centre of the table alongside the big bowl of rice, sweetcorn, and salad, then invite everyone to tuck in. For some extra flavour, cook the sweetcorn with one of my flavoured butters on pages 116–17.

FOR THE CHILLI

Serves 4

Prep time: 10–15 minutes

Cooking time: 20 minutes, or 2¼ hours if making ragu from scratch

INGREDIENTS

1 tbsp Hot and Smoky Spice Mix (see p.134) or smoked paprika

1 chilli, deseeded and chopped

2 tbsp rapeseed oil

500g (1lb 2oz) My Best Ragu (see p.64)

400g can kidney beans, drained

coriander, chopped chilli, lime wedges, and soured cream, to serve

1 In a large saucepan, fry the spice mix and the chilli in the oil for a minute then add the ragu and the kidney beans.

2 Simmer everything for 10 minutes until warmed through. If cooking the ragu from frozen, simply gently reheat for a bit longer until it is warmed through, about 20 minutes, and add a dash of water or stock if the ragu is a little thick or dries out. Serve in a large bowl with the coriander and chopped chilli scattered over and lime wedges and a pot of soured cream alongside.

FOR THE RICE

Serves 4

Prep time: 5 minutes

Cooking time: 20 minutes

INGREDIENTS

30g (1oz) butter

250g (9oz) mushrooms, sliced

2 red peppers, deseeded and finely sliced

200g (7oz) basmati or long-grain rice

2 garlic cloves, crushed

375ml (12½fl oz) hot chicken stock

1 To cook the rice, melt the butter in a pan. Add the mushrooms and peppers and cook for 2 minutes, until they are starting to soften. Stir in the rice and garlic and cook for another minute then pour over the stock.

2 Cover the pan with a lid and simmer gently for 8 minutes, then turn off the heat and leave the rice to steam for 10 minutes. Take off the lid and fluff the rice with a fork before serving in a large bowl alongside the other dishes.

FOR THE SWEETCORN

Serves 4

Prep time: 5 minutes

Cooking time: 6 minutes

INGREDIENTS

4 heads sweetcorn
30g (1oz) butter
1 chilli, deseeded and chopped
1 tbsp coriander, chopped
juice of 1 lime
salt and freshly ground black pepper

1 Cook the corn in boiling salted water for 5 minutes then drain and put the corn to one side. In the same pan, melt the butter and fry the chilli in the butter for 1 minute.

2 Return the corn to the pan and coat it in the butter, then sprinkle over the coriander and lime juice, season well, and serve alongside the chilli, rice, and salad.

FOR THE AVOCADO AND RED ONION SALAD

Serves 4

Prep time: 5 minutes

INGREDIENTS

2 medium avocados, pitted, flesh cut into cubes
½ red onion, very thinly sliced
1 tsp olive oil
juice of 1 lime
salt and freshly ground black pepper

1 Put the avocado in a bowl with all of the other ingredients, toss the ingredients together, and season well.

2 Serve the avocado and red onion salad alongside the chilli, rice, and the sweetcorn.

- MIDDLE EASTERN LAMB *Feast* -

I love richly spiced Middle Eastern food, it's perfect for sharing. Salads and hummus are served with lamb, fish, or meat dishes and delicious flatbreads. For this feast, try serving the flatbreads with the lamb, tabbouleh, and hummus, then let everyone help themselves to pomegranates, chilli, yogurt, and feta.

FOR THE LAMB

Serves 4–6

Prep time: 5–10 minutes

Cooking time: 10–15 minutes

INGREDIENTS

1 tbsp rapeseed oil

1 onion, finely chopped

1 tbsp Middle Eastern spice mix (see p.134), or 2 tsp smoked paprika and 1 tsp cinnamon

500g (1lb 2oz) lean minced lamb

1 garlic clove, chopped

salt and freshly ground black

peppermint and coriander leaves, to garnish

To serve

flatbreads – (see p.167) or use shop-bought flatbreads

pomegranate seeds

chilli, deseeded and chopped, to taste

thick Greek yogurt

75g (2½oz) feta, crumbled

1 Heat the oil in a large frying pan, add the onion, and cook for 5 minutes, or until the onion is softening and is starting to take on a bit of colour.

2 Add the spice mix and cook for another minute before tipping in the lamb and adding the garlic. Cook on a high heat for 5–6 minutes, breaking up the lamb with a wooden spoon, until it is well browned. Season with salt and pepper and top with a few peppermint and coriander leaves.

3 Serve the lamb in a large bowl alongside the tabbouleh and hummus. Lay out the flatbreads and either invite everyone to fill these with the different dishes, adding pomegranates, chilli, yogurt, and feta as desired, or simply help themselves to the dishes, using the flatbreads to mop everything up.

FOR THE TABBOULEH

Serves 4–6

Prep time: 10 minutes

Cooking time: 45 minutes

INGREDIENTS
75g (2½oz) bulgur wheat
30g (1oz) mint, finely chopped
100g (3½oz) flat-leaf parsley,
    finely chopped
150g (5½oz) tomatoes, deseeded
    and diced
4 spring onions, chopped
juice of 1 lemon
3 tbsp olive oil
salt and freshly ground black pepper

1 Rinse the bulgur wheat until the water runs clear, then place it in a bowl. Pour over 300ml (10fl oz) of boiling water, cover with cling film, and leave to soak for 45 minutes.

2 In the meantime, place the herbs in a bowl together with the tomatoes and spring onions. Drain the bulgur wheat well then add it to the bowl along with the lemon juice and the olive oil. Mix everything well, season with salt and pepper, and serve together with the lamb and hummus.

FOR THE GREEN HUMMUS

Serves 4–6

Prep time: 10 minutes

INGREDIENTS
400g can chickpeas, drained
1 garlic clove
4 tbsp chopped flat-leaf parsley
2 tbsp chopped chives
1 tbsp chopped tarragon
1 tbsp tahini (optional)
juice of 1 lemon
3 tbsp olive oil
salt and freshly ground black pepper

1 Place the chickpeas, garlic, herbs, tahini, if using, lemon juice, and oil in a food processor then blitz. Take the lid off and scrape off any mixture from the sides.

2 Blitz once more, adding a little water if the hummus is too thick. Once the hummus is a smooth texture, season with salt and pepper and serve alongside the rest of the feast dishes.

- Chinese PORK RIB Feast -

The addition of a fruity salsa gives this feast its oriental twist. The refreshing fruit cuts perfectly through the richness of the pork ribs. Serve the ribs in the middle of the table, with the egg-fried rice and mango salsa on the side, then encourage everyone to get stuck in!

FOR THE RIBS

Serves 4

Prep time: 40 minutes

Cooking time: 2 hours 15 minutes

INGREDIENTS
2 tbsp Chinese five-spice or paste

5cm (2in) piece ginger, roughly chopped

2 garlic cloves, sliced

1 red chilli, deseeded and chopped

4 tbsp oyster sauce

2 tbsp soy sauce

300ml (10fl oz) chicken stock

2 racks of baby back pork ribs

To serve
chilli, deseeded and chopped, to taste

coriander, chopped

lime wedges

1 Preheat the oven to 160°C (325°F/Gas 3). Place the five-spice, ginger, garlic, chilli, oyster sauce, soy sauce, and stock in a large roasting tray and mix everything together. Add the ribs and turn them over to coat them in the sauce then cover the tray with foil, pop it in the oven, and cook for 2 hours. Check the ribs occasionally to baste them in the sauce and make sure the meat isn't drying out – if it looks dry, just add some more stock or water.

2 Take the foil off and raise the oven temperature to 200°C (400°F/Gas 6). Cook for another 10–15 minutes, until the ribs are sticky and caramelized. Scatter the chilli and coriander over the ribs and put them on a large plate in the centre of the table with the lime wedges on the side, ready for everyone to help themselves.

FOR THE EGG-FRIED RICE

Serves 4

Prep time: 5 minutes

Cooking time: 8–10 minutes

INGREDIENTS

1 tbsp rapeseed oil

4 spring onions, chopped

500g (1lb 2oz) cooked rice, or 2 x 250g bags ready-cooked rice

50g (1¾oz) frozen peas, run under hot water for a minute

50g (1¾oz) frozen sweetcorn, run under hot water for a minute

2 eggs, beaten

2 tbsp soy sauce

1 tbsp sesame oil

1 Heat the oil in a large frying pan, add the spring onions and cook for a minute before adding the rice. Fry the rice for 2 minutes, scatter in the peas and sweetcorn, and fry for another couple of minutes, then push everything to one side of the pan.

2 Pour the beaten eggs into the clear side of the pan and mix them with a wooden spoon to break them up. Once they start to scramble, stir the rice back into the eggs until well combined. Season the rice with soy sauce and sesame oil and serve in a large bowl alongside the ribs and the salsa.

FOR THE MANGO SALSA

Serves 4

Prep time: 10 minutes

INGREDIENTS

1 large mango, ideally not very ripe, peeled, flesh removed from around the stone, and finely diced

1 chilli, deseeded and finely chopped

½ red onion, finely chopped

1 red pepper, deseeded and finely diced

2 tbsp coriander leaves

juice of 1 lime

1 tbsp fish or soy sauce

1 Mix all of the ingredients for the salsa together in a large bowl. If there is time, it's best to make the salsa a couple of hours before eating. Keep the salsa in the fridge then take it out about 10 minutes before serving to take the chill off it.

2 Serve the salsa alongside the ribs and the rice.

- PIZZA Party -

A pizza party may sound like a lot of work, but if you make up the dough the night before and leave it to rise in the fridge overnight you can save time on the day. You can also prep the other ingredients in advance if you wish, then all you'll need to do is roll out the dough, top the pizzas, and cook – simple!

FOR THE PIZZA DOUGH

Makes 4 thin pizzas

Prep time: 30 minutes, plus rising

INGREDIENTS

500g (1lb 2oz) strong white flour, plus extra for dusting
2 tsp salt
2 tsp caster sugar
1 x 7g sachet of dried yeast

1 To make the dough, place the flour in a large bowl. Sprinkle over the salt on one side, the sugar on the other side, and the yeast in the middle, then mix everything together.

2 Make a well in the centre of the flour and pour in 300ml (10fl oz) of lukewarm water. Using a fork, slowly start to mix the flour and water together, bringing the flour in from the sides. If the dough starts to feel a bit dry, just add a little more water. Once everything comes together to form a soft dough, tip it out onto a lightly floured work surface and knead for 5 minutes.

3 Place the dough in a clean bowl and cover with cling film. Put the dough in the fridge and leave it to rise for at least 2 hours until it has doubled in size, or leave it overnight if you are making the dough a day ahead.

FOR THE PIZZA TOPPINGS

Prep time: 20 minutes

Cooking time: 10 minutes

INGREDIENTS

Tomato Sauce (see 64) or passata seasoned with salt and freshly ground black pepper

2 balls of mozzarella, drained then left to sit on kitchen paper to remove excess water

Choice of toppings to go on before cooking

ham, salami and cold meats

selection of vegetables – choose from jarred artichokes, peppers, sliced mushrooms, courgette ribbons, red onion slices, blanched asparagus, fresh tomato or sundried tomatoes, frozen spinach, thawed with any excess water squeezed out

goat's cheese

red onion marmalade

chilli

olives

Choice of toppings for the cooked pizzas

rocket, pesto, watercress, basil, Parma ham, Parmesan shavings

1 Preheat the oven to 220°C (425°F/Gas 7). Divide the dough into 4 evenly sized balls and roll these out on a floured surface to form 4 thin discs.

2 Top each disc with the tomato sauce, pushing this to the sides, then invite everyone to scatter over their choice of toppings and tear over some mozzarella. Pizzas can be veggie-only, or a combination of a meat and two or three vegetables, with extras such as goat's cheese, marmalade, and chilli adding sweet, tangy, and spicy flavours, as preferred – aim for three or four toppings per pizza to avoid overloading them.

3 Bake the pizzas straight on a shelf in the oven for 10 minutes, or until golden and bubbling. Serve with the selection of toppings for everyone to choose from.

"

FAMILY FEASTS ARE MY ABSOLUTE FAVOURITE. *Everyone* TOGETHER ROUND THE TABLE. PERFECT!

"

- Build-Your-Own FAJITAS -

These beauties are messy! There's plenty of camaraderie while everyone is helping themselves – the table and your fingers will get sticky so have napkins at the ready! Place the chicken and the two salsas on the table with the tortilla wraps, ready for everyone to create their favourite fajita.

FOR THE CHICKEN

Serves 4 (2 wraps each)

Prep time: 10–15 minutes

Cooking time: 15 minutes

INGREDIENTS

2 tbsp rapeseed oil

2 onions, sliced

4 chicken breasts, skinless and
  boneless, thinly sliced

2 peppers, deseeded and sliced

2 tbsp Hot and Smoky Spice mix
  (see p.134)

To serve

8 tortilla wraps

200ml (7fl oz) soured cream

100g (3½oz) Cheddar, grated

lime wedges

1 Heat the oil in a large frying pan. Fry the onion for 5 minutes, until softened, then add the chicken, peppers, and spice mix.

2 Combine all the ingredients well so that the spices coat the chicken and peppers evenly. Fry for 2 minutes then add a tablespoon of water to stop the dish drying out. Cook for a further 3–5 minutes, depending on how thick the chicken is, then remove from the heat.

3 Place the chicken on the table next to the tortilla wraps, with the soured cream, Cheddar, and lime wedges in small bowls. Serve alongside the avocado and tomato salsas then invite everyone to fill their tortilla with their chosen toppings, wrap it all up, and enjoy!

FOR THE AVOCADO SALSA

Serves 4

Prep time: 5–10 minutes

INGREDIENTS

2 avocados, stones removed and cut into 1cm (½in) cubes

½ red onion, finely chopped

juice and zest of 1 lime

1 tbsp olive oil

pinch of chilli flakes or a little chopped chilli

salt and freshly ground black pepper

1 To make the avocado salsa, toss all the ingredients together and season with salt and pepper.

2 Serve the avocado salsa with the tortillas and the chicken and accompaniments.

FOR THE TOMATO SALSA

Serves 4

Prep time: 5 minutes

Cooking time: 5 minutes

INGREDIENTS

400g (14oz) cherry tomatoes, halved

1 tbsp caster sugar

1 tbsp vinegar

1 Use clean hands to squeeze the halved cherry tomatoes over a sieve so that some of the seeds are squeezed out, then set the tomatoes to one side.

2 Heat a small frying pan on a medium heat and sprinkle the sugar over the base of the pan. Allow the sugar to melt for a couple of minutes without stirring it, then once it is a light golden brown, tip in the tomatoes, standing back as they will spit at this stage. The sugar will harden again now. Add the vinegar and gently stir everything together, allowing the sugar to melt once more.

3 Cook for 3 minutes, until the sauce is slightly sticky and has thickened, then take the pan off the heat and leave to cool slightly. Serve the tomato salsa while still warm with the tortillas and the chicken and its accompaniments.

INDEX

ACKNOWLEDGMENTS

The author would like to thank
I have so many people to thank, not only for giving me the opportunity to write this book and help me do it, but also for helping me get to a position to even be able to write a book in the first place.

Firstly, I would like to thank all the wonderful team at Dorling Kindersley for giving me the opportunity and support to create this book; thank you for all your trust and help.

A big thank you to everyone at DML – Borra, for your wealth of expertise and knowledge; Jan for looking after me and all your endless support and for putting up with me; Louise for making sure I'm always in the right place at the right time; and Tang for all your hard work. You all go above and beyond for me time and again so thank you.

Gee Charman, for understanding my vision of this book. When I think back to our first meeting this is nothing short of a miracle. I can honestly say that I could not have done this without you and together we have created a book which I hope you will be as proud of as I am. I promise the next one *will* be easier!

I would also like to thank critically acclaimed author, friend, and mentor, Jo Scarrat Jones, for everything you do, and for always being there for me.

I would like to thank everyone at the BBC for seeing something in me. It still doesn't feel real. Alison Kirkham deserves a special mention for holding my hand and supporting me through this adventure.

I need to thank the team behind The Naked Grocer – without you guys none of this would be possible. My two brilliant sisters, Jacqui and Stephanie, thank you for your hard work and for believing in me; we can be very proud of what we achieved. Jeff Revell and Chris Stewart for not only being great friends, but for also giving up your time to help me – it will never be forgotten. Ozzie Hamblen for being the brains behind the brand; Tom Pratten for 26 years of friendship and for putting my ideas into practice; my sister- and brother-in-law, Abi and Gav, for the name and for all your help. And each and every one of you that worked in or shopped in The Naked Grocer. Thank you all for such an amazing time.

CONTINUED ▶

My Mum and Dad deserve a massive thank you for their love, support, and trust in me. I think I may well have tested the notion of unconditional love.

A huge thank you to my mother- and father-in-law, Gill and Alan, for all your endless support and help. I don't know how we could manage without you.

Two people that I have learnt a lot from are Clive Sluter and Rob Cullum; you have both been instrumental in my career and I'm proud to call you both friends.

Gregg Wallace, thank you for helping and advising me in my new career, you have been brilliant.

I would like to thank my two very very special boys. Thank you for giving me perspective, drive, and ambition; my proudest achievement is being your Daddy. They also deserve a mention for some first-rate modelling skills and for helping to create some of the recipes.

I reserve my last thank you to my incredible wife and partner. Thank you for everything – you are my rock, my sounding board, my sanity, my world, and none of this would be possible without you. Thank you for keeping me grounded and focused, for your love and support, and for being the best mum to our children.

The publisher would like to thank
Philippa Dawson for proofreading; Hilary Bird for the index; Steve Crozier for image retouching; Lucy Patchett and Victoria Barnes for hair and make-up

ABOUT THE AUTHOR

Chris Bavin enjoys a busy career as a BBC TV presenter. He has co-presented four series of *Eat Well for Less* with Gregg Wallace; appeared as a judge on *Britain's Best Home Cook* alongside Mary Berry and Dan Doherty; was a presenter on *Tomorrow's Food* and the documentaries *The Truth About Meat* and *The Truth About Obesity*; and is a presenter on *Food: Truth or Scare*.

Chris's background is in the food industry, where he has worked for over 20 years. He started by importing fruit and vegetables from all over the world and selling it to the wholesale markets. He found wholesale markets incredible places and loved how they operated through the night, selling fruit and vegetables to the greengrocers, barrow boys, retail markets, and restaurants. He fell in love with the people, the business, and the amazing produce.

In 2009, Chris opened a greengrocer's called *The Naked Grocer*. This gave him in-depth knowledge of fresh produce and helped him to understand what produce people liked to buy and why. He twice won Independent Retailer of the Year.

As well as his busy TV career, Chris gives cookery demonstrations and delivers educational talks to children, where he hopes to pass on his passion for good food.